P9-BZU-035

ON 𝔐OZART
A Paean for Wolfgang

ALSO BY ANTHONY BURGESS

Novels
The Long Day Wanes
    Time for a Tiger
    The Enemy in the Blanket
    Beds in the East
The Right to an Answer
The Doctor Is Sick
The Worm and the Ring
Devil of a State
One Hand Clapping
A Clockwork Orange
The Waning Seed
Honey for the Bears
Inside Mr. Enderby
Nothing like the Sun: A Story of Shakespeare's Love-Life
The Eve of Saint Venus
A Vision of Battlements
Tremor of Intent
Enderby Outside
MF
Napoleon Symphony
The Clockwork Testament or, Enderby's End
Beard's Roman Women
Abba Abba
Man of Nazareth
1985
Earthly Powers
The End of the World News
Enderby's Dark Lady
The Kingdom of the Wicked
The Pianoplayers
Any Old Iron

For Children
A Long Trip to Teatime
The Land Where the Ice Cream Grows

Verse
Moses

Nonfiction
English Literature: A Survey for Students
They Wrote in English
Language Made Plain
Here Comes Everybody: An Introduction to James Joyce for
    the Ordinary Reader
The Novel Now: A Student's Guide to Contemporary Fiction
Urgent Copy: Literary Studies
Shakespeare
Joysprick: An Introduction to the Language of James Joyce
New York
Hemingway and His World
On Going to Bed
This Man and Music
Ninety-Nine Novels
Flame into Being
    The Life and Works of D. H. Lawrence
Little Wilson and Big God
You've Had Your Time

Translator
The New Aristocrats
The Olive Trees of Justice
The Man Who Robbed Poor Boxes
Cyrano de Bergerac
Oedipus the King

Editor
The Grand Tour
Coaching Days of England
A Shorter Finnegans Wake

On
𝕸𝖔𝖟𝖆𝖗𝖙

A Paean for Wolfgang

Being a celestial colloquy, an opera libretto, a
film script, a schizophrenic dialogue, a bewildered rumination, a Stendhalian transcription,
and a heartfelt homage upon the bicentenary of
the death of Wolfgang Amadeus Mozart

Anthony Burgess

Ticknor & Fields
NEW YORK
1991

Copyright © 1991 by Anthony Burgess

ALL RIGHTS RESERVED

For information about permission to reproduce selections
from this book, write to Permissions, Ticknor & Fields,
Houghton Mifflin Company, 2 Park Street, Boston,
Massachusetts 02108.

Library of Congress Cataloging-in-Publication Data
Burgess, Anthony, date.
On Mozart : a paean for Wolfgang / Anthony Burgess.
p.   cm.
ISBN 0-395-59510-X
1. Imaginary conversations.   2. Mozart, Wolfgang Amadeus,
1756–1791—Drama.   3. Music.   I. Title.
PR6052.U63805   1991   91-22878
822'.914—dc20   CIP

Printed in the United States of America

Book design by Robert Overholtzer

BP 10 9 8 7 6 5 4 3 2 1

Nineteen ninety-one, the year of the bicentenary of Mozart's death, has already been celebrated with due devotion and even mindless awe. Here was the supreme musical genius, whose works may be analyzed by the expert without elucidating their true nature, and whose life has been presented so often, in book and in film, that it would be foolish to retell the story yet again. This tribute has an ironic component. The scene is set mostly in heaven, from which Saddam Hussein's guns can be faintly heard. I split Anthony Burgess up into several warring historical personages and initiate discussions which get nowhere except a region where an understanding of the nature of music (not just Mozart's) may conceivably begin to dawn. Mozart brings solace to our tattered lives, but he also brings bewilderment. This is, in fact, a bewildered book, in which an attempt to understand Mozart is made through celestial dialogue, a Stendhalian effort at turning Symphony No. 40 into fiction, an opera libretto, and fragments of a film script; these various forms join with the author's own schizophrenia to answer the unanswerable: in effect, the meaning of music. The centennial year has not seen a more original, lively, diverse and annoying homage to the greatest of the world's composers.

ON $\mathfrak{M}$OZART
A Paean for Wolfgang

Prologue

BEETHOVEN:

Is that gunfire down there?

MENDELSSOHN:

Who are you? Oh, I see. Dignified, kempt, all of eighty or ninety. I prefer the tempestuous appearance, the peering desperateness of the very deaf. I beg you, be the Beethoven we know from the icons.

BEETHOVEN:

Time enough. Eternity all too much. Is that gunfire down there?

MENDELSSOHN:

Yes, and worse. There seems to be a war on.

BEETHOVEN:

Dona nobis pacem. You know the *Missa Solemnis?*

MENDELSSOHN:

Not one of my favorite works. The sopranos screech.

BEETHOVEN:

Not in the inner performance which was all I had. A slight miscalculation. I always overestimated the capacities of women. Under the *Dona nobis pacem* I had a menacing trumpet and drum. Meaning that only up here would we ever get a genuine *pacem*. Who is it this time?

MENDELSSOHN:

There is some Muslim madman or other screeching for a holy war. Islam has changed from my day, yours. It offered more decorative concepts. Arabesques. And, of course, the jingling johnnies of the janissaries.

BEETHOVEN:

So the Turks are at it again. They left one good thing behind when they ran away from Vienna — a bag of coffee beans. The coffee up here is damnably weak.

MENDELSSOHN:

Meaning heavenly so. We are past the need for stimulation. It's not the Turks, by the way.

BEETHOVEN:

That stupid canon of Haydn runs through my head sometimes. K A F F E E. Two bars of three-four. And then something about *Sei keiner Mussulman*. Where is Haydn these days?

MENDELSSOHN:

Revising *The Creation*. He's been given some inside information about that process. As I say, it's not the Turks. The action emanates from Baghdad. The chief aim seems to be the liquidation of the Jewish people.

BEETHOVEN:

I thought we'd had all that. Well, you, not me. It's about fifty years of earth time since you put on that silly skullcap and started to learn Hebrew. When they started killing the Jews you suddenly decided to be a Jew. The prick of ancestry. A lot of nonsense.

MENDELSSOHN:
I merely emulate our supreme lord and director. He who singularized himself from the plural *Elohim* and became Jehovah. Even heaven is tinged by racism. He grew tired of being the mere *élan vital*. The universe owes everything to the Jews.

BEETHOVEN:
Have you visited that region where the Turks are?

MENDELSSOHN:
Not just Turks. As I say, Islam has become a wider concept since our time. Yes, I had a look. Houris and sherbet and a running river. And the tribal offshoot of the deity they call Allah beaming through his beard. The Old Man of the Mountains is what they call him. He doles out rations of hashish. Not my sort of thing at all. I prefer haggis. After all, the Scots are a kind of Jew.

BEETHOVEN:
These Turks or whatever they are have an intolerable music. No harmony, no counterpoint. Everything wailed in unison. I should imagine that all Semitic music is the same. Not that I hear much of it. I make myself deaf when the Lord orders one of his heavenly concerts. Would you truly call yourself a Semitic musician?

MENDELSSOHN:
That mad German sect thought so. Smashed my statues, threw my scores onto a bonfire, banned even my Scottish works from their stupid concerts. No, I accept that I am nothing without my Western inheritance. Which, of course, is Christian, even ecclesiastical. The Jewish aspect encompasses energy, imagination,

belief in the sacred nature of the family, devotion to the community at large. I composed music for the delectation of the communal ear.

BEETHOVEN:
So did I, even though I could not myself hear it. So do they all.

MENDELSSOHN:
Not all. Some have composed and still compose to exasperate the public ear. I regret to say that they are usually Jews.

BEETHOVEN:
You were always too bland. You never dared enough.

MENDELSSOHN:
I resent that.

BEETHOVEN:
Ach, we're past resentment here. We're supposed to be glorified. We're considered to be past the diseases of time. But what is eternity? The split second prolonged. Acceptable to saints and mystics but not to musicians. Thanks to Him up there we have musical time if not clock time. All right, resent if you wish to. And, speaking of resentment, I'm sick of this decor you've set up for yourself — Balmoral Castle or somewhere with Fingal's cave outside the window. Do you object to my changing it to the Viennese woods?

MENDELSSOHN:
This is my personal patch of infinity. If you don't like it —

BEETHOVEN:
I came here because you seem to have taken on certain organizational duties which cover the arrangement of centennial tributes. Ach, who are these?

PROKOFIEV:

Sergei Prokofiev, born 1891.

BLISS:

Sir Arthur Bliss. Same year. Master of the Queen's Musick.

BEETHOVEN:

I regret to say that I do not know either of you. You've kept your distance up to now. You are Russian?

PROKOFIEV:

Russian born. Then a citizen of the world. But the homeland called. I served the Soviet Union. At present in the process of rapid disintegration. I did my best. I resent nothing. Except perhaps not being Beethoven.

BEETHOVEN:

Ach, they all resent that. Even Mendelssohn here. You, sir, seem to be a soldier, not a musician.

BLISS:

I was an officer in one of the world wars. I've gone back to the uniform, complete with decorations. I understood that there was to be an official celebration of my birth.

PROKOFIEV:

I think you have made a small mistake there, comrade, *cher maître*, whatever you wish to be called.

MENDELSSOHN:

Look, I resent your saying that I resent not being yourself. Pardon me, gentlemen. There is a certain assumption on the part of our fellow composer Ludwig van Beethoven that he represents the musical pinnacle. I concede his virtues — chiefly what that great Scot Sir Walter terms the big bowwow style — but I'm appalled by his vices — a clumsiness in his use of orchestra, the intrusion of ego, a total lack of the graces of femininity —

BEETHOVEN:
Do you expect femininity from one who may have lost his ears but maintained a firm possession of his —

MENDELSSOHN:
Do not say it. I execrate your Dutch coarseness. A composer, indeed any artist, must be a kind of hermaphrodite.

BLISS:
Like the Royal Marines. Ermophrodite. A popular deformation borrowed by Kipling.

MENDELSSOHN:
Delicacy. Elegance. Restraint. Music suitable for Shakespeare's fairies. There is more to the art than storm and stress and thundery bluster.

PROKOFIEV:
Surely this is unseemly? There is a time and place for everything, even when time and place have ceased to be viable concepts. Although I confess that it was a keeping of earthly time that brought me to this secretariat. I understood that I was to be celebrated.

BLISS:
You already are, and perhaps more than you ought to be. You abased yourself before the bloodthirsty Stalin. You placed the philistine state before the call of your individual talent.

PROKOFIEV:
I resent that.

BEETHOVEN:

There seems to be a lot of resentment going on this heavenly day. You, sir, captain or major or whatever you are, what sort of musician do you claim to be?

BLISS:

British. English, if you prefer. If there is resentment to be expressed, my own is directed at the fact of my nationality, or rather the musical culture under which my nation has suffered. You Germans, from Handel on, have dominated it. You, Herr Mendelssohn, kept the Victorian age in servitude to a bland and wishy-washy orthodoxy which only the powerful personality of Edward Elgar and the later revival of the folkish modal tradition were able to drive out. You kept us far behind the European currents of musical progress.

BEETHOVEN:

What nonsense! Music does not progress. Handel knew neither the augmented sixth nor the Neapolitan one, but there is no music greater. My personal resentment is that I am not Handel. I have viewed that giant two or three times, though he does not wish to be visited. He conserves his blindness even in this afterworld and consumes vast phantom meals. He will not discuss music. He says he wrote it only to make money. He is not happy in heaven. He wants the candlewax stink of theaters and quarrels with castrati. Nor will he admit his own greatness.

BLISS:

He wrote great tunes. Perhaps that is all that music is really about. Great tunes. We do not go to either of you two German gentlemen for great tunes. You, sir, wrote a fine wedding march and you, sir, a moderately singable theme to match Schiller's ode, but only the soil of England has ever succeeded in sprouting great tunes. That is why I gravitated from the prickly avantgarde towards Elgarian nobility. And, as we are still talking of resentment, you must all admit to resenting Elgar.

BEETHOVEN:
We do not know him. Wait, there is a song that is sung in that English *Bierstube* —

BLISS:
We call it a pub. That is an abbreviation for "public house." The drinks served are celestial, meaning they lack body. But the singing is full-bodied enough. The customers, who insist on paying celestial money and receiving celestial change, sometimes sing "Land of Hope and Glory." The words are trivial but the melody most noble. It is the trio of a march that Elgar wrote. Perhaps that tune is not really exportable, except to heaven. On holiday in Italy I heard it, true, but as a background to a television commercial for Twining's tea. There is, by the way, no drinkable tea here except in the self-elected Irish ghetto. But there is too much fighting there. The Irish heaven seems to be perpetual combat.

BEETHOVEN:
What is television?

BLISS:
It is the resurrection of the body. The dead live on it.

MENDELSSOHN:
You talk of unexportability. But the whole point of music is that it breaks Babel. It is the one universal human language. The failure of a composer to transcend national barriers has nothing to do with the soil from which he grows. If the world rejects a composer, it is because his voice is too weak to carry.

PROKOFIEV:
The music of Russia is Russia herself.

BEETHOVEN:
I do not wish to know Russia. Well, the odd count or prince in

exile perhaps. A little caviar on black bread. There is an interesting point I would raise now. It is this. Here we are speaking our native tongues which, by some celestial device, are immediately converted into the language of the listeners. Consider now —

PROKOFIEV:
That is called simultaneous translation. A Soviet invention.

BEETHOVEN:
Now, music too is a language, but an untranslatable one. And it is true, despite what Rabbi Mendelssohn says, that it has nationalistic elements which hinder its universal transmission. Here, in this place of ultimate reality, one would expect the barriers to break, but they do not. You, sir, talk of English music. I once wrote variations on your "God Save the King" —

BLISS:
At present it is "God Save the Queen." But it is the same tune.

BEETHOVEN:
It is English, but why is it English? It is only notes.

BLISS:
There is something behind the notes which not even God — saving His near presence — can elucidate. Elgar himself, glorified though he is, cannot explain why his symphonic poem *Falstaff* conjures visions of the Worcestershire apple orchards.

BEETHOVEN:
You seem to place Elgar above God.

BLISS:
In matters of music he is. God does not understand music. Indeed, God seems to hate music. That was always Elgar's view. The first performance of his *Dream of Gerontius* was a terrible

fiasco, and he blamed God for it. That is why he refuses to attend any of the divine levees. He does not wish to meet God. He is content to put celestial money on celestial horses at the celestial Derby and other race meetings. He would prefer God to be a horse.

MENDELSSOHN:
Like that mad dean who is worshiped by the more sober of the Irish.

PROKOFIEV:
You talk of God, and I caught a glimpse of God on my arrival here. But I still cling to my atheism. The concept of an omnipotent being is exploded, I think, by the fact that God cannot play a musical instrument, much less compose. God has no hands.

BEETHOVEN:
Proving that hands are a negative property. But I hear reports that God, in His infinite wisdom and humility, has grown hands temporarily. Mozart proposes to teach Him the harpsichord.

BLISS:
I have seen nothing of Mozart since I came here.

MENDELSSOHN:
Mozart is supposed to be the being closest to God. And this terrestrial year his bicentenary is to be celebrated. Whether he can be persuaded to leave the divine presence is not yet clear. Nevertheless, I have the responsibility of arranging certain major events in honor of his genius. You two gentlemen are, I fear, unlucky. The year of Mozart's death has an effulgence that throws into dark shadow your common year of birth. We lesser musicians must bow down to him on this occasion.

PROKOFIEV:
What is proposed?

MENDELSSOHN:
All the works.

PROKOFIEV:
That goes too far. Some are of very nugatory importance.

MENDELSSOHN:
Also an opera, not by Mozart, in which Mozart is the leading character. Ah, here comes the man who turned opera into unbearable Teutonic epic. The reek of his French perfume announces his coming like a vulgar unison of cornets.

WAGNER:
I hear you, Jew.

MENDELSSOHN:
Thank our Jewish God that I do not have to hear *you*. Have you yet managed to drag an audience into your celestial *Schauspielhaus*?

WAGNER:
It is enough to ravish the soul of Ludwig.

BEETHOVEN:
I object to your familiarity. Your lying familiarity.

WAGNER:
I referred to another Ludwig. The King of Bavaria, my adorer.

BLISS:
Still mad, then?

WAGNER:
Who is this impertinent soldier?

BLISS:

Bliss, transported to bliss. Sir Arthur. A composer.

WAGNER:

English. Any stretto-wangling pedant in your country is made a knight. What is this I hear about some Mozart celebration? Much as I appreciate his mellifluities, despite their limitations, do we not already celebrate him enough? His divertimenti regale our dinner parties, his quartets resound in our billiard rooms. God pets him overmuch. God has to be reminded occasionally that he is really not the periwigged deity of baroque Austrian chapels.

MENDELSSOHN:

In the sense that God can only be defined as God, so the music of Mozart can only be defined as music. Some say he was the last composer to distill music's pure essence. We tolerate the limitations because of that truth. With all due respect to Herr Beethoven, the rot began in his Fifth Symphony. Nonmusical pollutants intruded. What does that unbarred oboe solo mean in the first movement? It means: here am I, the suffering Beethovenian soul, speaking to you. Mozart never committed so barbaric an indiscretion. I tried to restore the purity but failed. My music is too palpably *about* something. As for you, the non-Jew Wagner, you completed the destruction. You always had a vulgar soul.

WAGNER:

I will not have this!

MENDELSSOHN:

Oh, put off that stupid Gothic disguise. You are not a seven-foot Siegfried but a little man with no neck. You wrenched music into a political arena. You made it pornographic. You perverted it into the service of half-baked notions of Teutonic superiority.

WAGNER:

Did you not disguise your own Jewishness to pose as a Teuton? Did your grandfather Moses Mendelssohn not embrace Teutonic culture? True, I put music in its proper place, as the handmaiden of human emotions and progressive ideas. You merely purveyed picture postcards of the Scottish highlands and the more accessible street sights of a tourist's Italy. You played fairies. I at least was not a sentimental Jew.

PROKOFIEV:

You have only one chord. You hammered to death the secondary seventh on the leading note. The leading note of the dominant.

WAGNER:

Another pedant.

PROKOFIEV:

No. One who served the people's state with music they understood. One who put off decadent individualism to embrace a populist language. One who suffered.

WAGNER:

Do not talk to me of suffering, whoever you are. I was the archetypal sufferer.

PROKOFIEV:

And you passed on that suffering to your listeners. In our Great Patriotic War we fought against you and no other. You made yourself the incarnate voice of Teutonic arrogance.

WAGNER:

If I thought it would be of any use I would write pamphlets against the lot of you. War in heaven. Who could ever have believed that your transfiguration should fail to purge your grosser imbecilities? I do not, of course, include you, Herr Beethoven, in my commination.

BEETHOVEN:
No. I have already been purged. I was Catholic enough to have to undergo a period of catharsis.

BLISS:
I thought purgatory was merely an invention of Dante Alighieri.

BEETHOVEN:
Oh, it is real enough to the believer. It was not unpleasant. Mozart was already there when I descended into those regions of mild fire. We both had to repent of our freemasonry. Of our lust. Of jealousy, cupidity and other minor vices. It did not take long.

BLISS:
There is surely nothing sinful about freemasonry. Some great Englishmen have attained mastership in the lodges.

BEETHOVEN:
It was really the masonic music we composed that required our penitence. It was not good music. The key of E-flat was termed the masonic key. Clarinets the masonic instruments. Thirds and sixths the masonic intervals. Our rabbi is right when he says that music should not serve anything but itself. Mozart failed in purity there.

PROKOFIEV:
Surely *The Magic Flute* is masonic music?

BEETHOVEN:
It suggests secret societies and magical passwords. But it is bigger than any sectarian philosophy. One other thing I insisted on

expiating, though I was advised that there was no need, was the composition of my Ninth Symphony.

ALL:
What?

BEETHOVEN:
Oh yes, that damnable hybrid. That set back the Mozartian ideal of purity forever. It would have politicized music had I glorified that original key word of Schiller's. *Freiheit*, freedom, not *Freude*, joy. At least if I had hymned freedom it would have given those National Socialists pause. But joy can be joy in anything — in shoving Jews into gas ovens; in burning the works of your esteemed self, rabbi; in butchering Slavs, Gypsies and sexual inverts; in turning a Linz housepainter into a god. What could be more stupid than to praise a mere euphoria consequent on any possible action? That stupidity was sin enough. The other sin was to have musical instruments pretending to be inferior to the human voice. They sing of eternity, but an overfed baritone bids them sing of the pleasure of torturing Jews.

MENDELSSOHN:
You go too far, master.

WAGNER:
Without your glorious Ninth I could never have conceived of the Wagnerian music drama.

BEETHOVEN:
Relate music to human concepts and you end up making it imitate mere objects. That damnable Richard Strauss who was your follower has voiced untenable imbecilities. He deserved hell, if hell existed instead of being a mere laughable fiction, the salt and mustard of our bland bliss. When this Strauss expressed the desire of homage to me, I thought at first he was Johann Strauss,

composer of most tuneful waltzes. But he was of a different family, named for you, Wagner, and he said that music could have what he called real-life referents. He said that music could represent knives, forks and spoons, and it should be possible to tell if those implements were made of cast iron or pewter.

WAGNER:

You say this is an imbecility? But the leitmotif of my music dramas is conceived on that assumption. Musical notes can be a river, a sword, a funeral pyre, a horse.

BLISS:

Not self-evidently. You have to label them first. You have to say this is this and that is that. A colleague of mine, a Lancastrian named Sir William Walton —

WAGNER:

Another of these benighted English knights.

BLISS:

He has a biblical oratorio called *Belshazzar's Feast*. In it various heathen gods are praised — the god of wood, of brass, of silver, of iron. For the iron an anvil, for the wood a xylophone, for the silver high woodwind and glockenspiel. This is legitimate, since he has words sung by the chorus naming the gods. But without those words we would guess nothing.

BEETHOVEN:

You see? The verbal heresy.

BLISS:

Hardly a heresy. Music began as verbal intonation. The separation of words and music may be regarded as the true heresy. Opera may well be the highest of the arts. Everything is there. Everything is a servant of everything else, and so everything achieves mastery. Let us not speak of the purity of Mozart when we have *Don Giovanni*.

MENDELSSOHN:
A proposito. Our heavenly time is flexible, but I have to invoke clock time to achieve synchronicity. I mean that an opera is due to commence. See, I change the scene to an opera house that combines the best of the earthly capitals. The audience is assembling. Mozart is not present in that special box. He is closeted with his maker. But all that matter are here.

WAGNER:
But who is the composer? Who the librettist?

MENDELSSOHN:
Blessed spirits who have shed their names with their bodies.

PROKOFIEV:
And the title?

MENDELSSOHN:
They have not thought of one yet.

Act One

An indeterminate hall in the Vienna palace of the Prince Arch-bishop Hieronymus Colleredo of Salzburg. Servants, male and fe-male, scrub, clean, polish, bring logs for the fireplace. Mozart, the court musician, warms himself gloomily.

SERVANTS:
Humble humble humble humble
Servants of his princely grace,
Fashed and fagged we groan and grumble,
Outcasts of the human race.
Humble humble humble humble
Burdened beasts that know their place.
See us fumble, see us stumble,
See the bitter bread we crumble
And the skilly that we mumble.
Dare to look us in the face,
Helots of his high disgrace.
Hear our empty bellies rumble
Treble
Alto
Tenor
Bass.

MOZART (*tenor*):
Slavishly begot,
Slavery's your lot.

Luggers in of logs,
You are less than dogs.
Dogs at least are fed
Bones as well as bread.
Lowly born,
Accept my scorn.

SERVANTS:
Humbly humbly humbly humbly
May we ask if it's a crime
Dumbly dumbly dumbly dumbly
(Yes, we know that's not a rhyme)
To be born beneath a star
Burning with malignant fire?
Humbly dumbly we inquire
Who the hell you think you are.

MOZART:
I was not born beneath a star. I
Am a star.
Leaning across the heavenly bar, I
Fell too far.
The crown of music on my head was
Knocked awry.
Fingering keys to earn my bread was
By and by
Ordained to be the life I led and
Still must lead.
So will it go till I am dead and
Dead indeed.

SERVANTS:
Humbly humbly humbly humbly
May we ask you what you mean?
All you said was soft and crumbly;
Words should cut as keen and clean

As the whip the gruff and grumbly
Majordomo, rough and rumbly,
Lays on us to vent his spleen.

MOZART:
I played the harpsichord at four
And scribbled symphonies at five.
I played and played from shore to shore.
I labored — never bee in hive
Buzzed harder at its sticky store —
To keep the family alive.
For Leopold, my father, swore
I'd fiddle, tinkle, sweat and strive
Until the name the family bore
Should gather honor and survive
Two centuries and even more.
But infant prodigies arrive
At puberty. Must we deplore
Our beards and balls, though noses dive
And patrons stay away or snore?
I serve His Highness now, contrive
To play the postures of a whore.
Too meanly paid to woo or wive,
I sink and sink who used to soar.
Grant me your pity, friends, for I've
Heard slam that ever-open door,
Been forced to kiss the nether floor,
Who once kissed queens —

SERVANTS:
Kissed queens?

MOZART:
Kissed queens.
Not anymore, not anymore.

My scullion companions, I've run out of hope. Also rhymes. To work. I hear steel heels and the crack of a whip.

Enter Majordomo and the Prince Archbishop's Private Secretary.

SERVANTS (*working*):
Humble humble humble humble
Servants of his princely grace,
Hear our empty bellies rumble
Treble
Alto
Tenor
Bass.

MAJORDOMO:
Scum. Go on. Hard at it.

SECRETARY:
Mozart.

MOZART:
That is my name.

SECRETARY:
Fifty new contredanses were ordered for the next court ball. Fifteen only have been delivered. The Te Deum for the impending return to Salzburg of His Grace has still to be composed. And the flute exercises for His Grace's nephew are awaited with impatience.

MOZART:
Surely you mean His Grace's oldest bastard.

SECRETARY:
Insolence, insolence.

MOZART:
Perhaps, but I know that His Grace is an only child. His mother's
womb bore once and once only. To have produced siblings to
compete with His Holy Uniqueness would have been the true
insolence.

SECRETARY:
I let that float past me as flatulent air. If you seek dismissal
through my mediacy you will not get it. You have been paid for
work not yet done. Do it.

MOZART:
Music cannot be ordered like a pound of tripe. But it will be
done. It is being done now. In my head. But I hope the Te Deum
can be postponed a month or more. Why will he not stay in
Vienna?

SECRETARY:
His responsibility is to Salzburg.

MOZART:
There is no place like Vienna.

The dust of Vienna,
The lust of Vienna
Swirls round my brain.
Erotic phantasmas
And putrid miasmas
That rise from each drain.
Its filth is creative,
The stink of each native
Olfactory song.
So I wish to stay here
And I wish to play here.
It's where I belong.

SECRETARY (*baritone*):
But Salzburg is pretty
And it is no pity
There's little to do.
A munch at an apple,
A prayer in the chapel
Should satisfy you.
Erotic temptation
And free fornication
Pass everyone by,
And it is no wonder
For everything's under
His Highness's eye.

MOZART:
A heavenly committee

Designed this hellish city
Full of joy.
Where even the decrepit
Joins the dance and learns to
    step it
Like a boy.
The pace is hot and hellish
But we savor it with relish

In this town.
Its poets ought to pen a
Panegyric, for Vienna
Wears the crown.
Vienna Vienna Vienna
Wears the crown.

SECRETARY:
Though neither wise nor
    witty,
Yet Salzburg's wholesome citi-
Zens employ
Their time in contemplation
Of their ultimate salvation

And annoy
Those immigrants of devils
Who would implement their
    revels
In this town.
O city crammed with virtue,
Let me sturdily assert: you
Wear the crown.
Salzburg Salzburg Salzburg
Wears the crown.

MOZART:
And, moreover, Vienna is the city of the fortepiano. The crashing
keyboard, the sustentive pedal. I could make my mark here.

SECRETARY:
The harpsichord is good enough for Salzburg. Stick to your tinkling, sir. I must away to my duties. Take pen, take paper, compose.

A clock strikes.

SECRETARY:
The physician is late. When he arrives, send him at once to His Highness.

He leaves. The Majordomo whips all the servants off except one, Lorenzo, who is small, dark and unsubdued. He polishes a classical statue of no great beauty or value.

MOZART:
I shall intermit the inner flute, sir, and do as you bid. (*He sings to himself, as follows*)
The piano, the piano,
Its limitless soprano,
Its thunder-making bass —
I'll look but never be bored
When seated at its keyboard.
A yawn will split my face,
Disdainful, autocratic,
As I range through its chromatic
Improbabilities,
Dashing off a new concerto
While the Viennese assert "Oh,
What a genius he is" . . .

Dr. Trapassi arrives, in a great hurry.

DR. TRAPASSI:
Your servant, maestro. Yes, I know I'm late. A little matter of a child with a toy stuck in his throat. What we medicos term the ingurgitation of an artifact.

MOZART:
How is His Highness?

DR. TRAPASSI:
Oh, well enough. He can go back to Salzburg tomorrow. But he requires another opinion. The Tabib Hakim should be here any moment now. A Turk, I regret to say. But His Highness has a superstitious faith in Constantinapolitan medicine. Be good enough to tell him where to go. I must hurry.

He rushes off, leaving his cloak and hat on the statue that Lorenzo is lazily polishing.

MOZART:
Lorenzo, you were once a prisoner of the Turks. You speak their language?

LORENZO:
A little bit, effendi.

MOZART:
Here are a few small coins. All I have. Wear that hat, that cloak. Proceed to His Highness's bedchamber. You are now a Turkish doctor. Turn him over, turn him upside down, if need be. Pummel him with vigor. Shake your head and indicate that he must stay here in Vienna and take your Turkish medicines. I will send away the real Tabib Hakim, telling him that he is not, after all, required. *Capito?*

LORENZO:
Si, effendi.

Lorenzo goes off gleefully, hatted and cloaked. Mozart resumes his song.

MOZART:
The piano, the piano,
The new career I plan, oh,
What lucre it will bring.
The *nuances* that I'll treadle
While my left foot on the pedal
Quietens down the triple string.
Then the crash as I release it
And the noise as I increase it
And the high harmonics sing
Will court the court's good temper, a
Feast to make the Emperor
As happy as a king.

Halfway through, the Turkish doctor enters. Mozart makes dismissive gestures.

MOZART:
His Highness has changed his mind. As well as his diet. You are
not wanted, effendi.

The Turk shrugs and departs. From the opposite door the Majordomo enters, beating Lorenzo viciously.

MAJORDOMO (*bass*):
I will beat you black and blue
Till your vertebrae shine through.
I will beat your wretched pate
Till your brains coagulate.

LORENZO (*bass*):
I meant no harm, sir.
Let go my arm, sir.
Only a joke, sir.
Sorry I spoke, sir.

MAJORDOMO:
Do not argue, do not speak.
Bread and skilly for a week.
Filthy water in your cup
And you'll take it standing up.

LORENZO:
Ow and then ow, sir.
Not speaking now, sir.
Ow. I am dumb, sir.
Merely a drum, sir.

MAJORDOMO:
Drums are only made of skin.
There's an emptiness within.
Underworked and overfed,
Belly crammed with beef and bread —

MAJORDOMO:
Fed with the Archbishop's food,
Thus you show your gratitude.
Shut your filthy orifice.
Take that and that and this and this.

LORENZO:
Ow, sir and ow, sir.

Quite enough now, sir.

Ready to drop, sir.
Beg you to stop, sir.

MOZART:
Yes, stop.

LORENZO:
Never said a word. Never got near His High Holiness.

MOZART:
Loyalty will get its reward.

MAJORDOMO:
You keep out of this, fiddler. Or were you in it?

MOZART:
You're a beast and bully. And you stink. The effluvium from your armpits makes me retch. Your mouth is a sewer. The blast of your garlicky breath would make a whole regiment retreat.

MAJORDOMO:
Why, you gut scraper, I'll have you. Remember what you are and what I am. I'll pull your moth-eaten periwig off and make better music on your unwashed scalp.

They start to tussle when two ladies appear. They are Aloysia and Constanze Weber.

ALOYSIA:
Really.

The two men desist.

MOZART:
It cannot be. Aloysia — what are you doing here? Your servant, madame.

MAJORDOMO:
Who shall I announce?

ALOYSIA:
Aloysia Weber, distinguished singer, and her sister Constanze, distinguished accompanist.

CONSTANZE:
Accompanists are not distinguished. Or rather distinguishable by being undistinguished.

ALOYSIA:
Reserve your wit for a more distinguished occasion, Constanze.
Go, announce us, fellow.

*Grumbling quietly, the Majordomo leaves. So, groaning, does
Lorenzo.*

MOZART:
It's all of four years. It was at Mannheim, was it not?

ALOYSIA:
I can't be sure. There are so many places. The Prince Archbishop of Salzburg expressed a desire to hear me sing while he
and I were both in Vienna. He is ravished by a certain aria recently composed by the great Salieri.

Mozart groans quietly at the name.

MOZART:
I will accompany you. Accompaniment is one of my duties here.

ALOYSIA:
I see. You are still a servant. You look like a servant. Can you
not afford better clothes?

MOZART:
A servant of my muse, Aloysia. And yes, visibly an underpaid
one. But surely you heard my opera *Idomeneo* at Munich?

ALOYSIA:
I was singing at Frankfurt, with great success. But I heard of
your *Idomeneo*. The arias were said to be too long.

MOZART:
The fault of that swine Metastasio. He refused to allow one

word to be cut. A bloody idiot when he's allowed in a theater.
I beg your pardon.

ALOYSIA:
As coarse as ever.

MOZART:
But still a most delicate musician. If His Highness wishes you to
sing, I have better music than Salieri's.

CONSTANZE:
It seems I am not really needed. And I know you have — ha! —
certain private things to say to my sister, Herr Mozart. I will go
back to our lodgings and wait on Father. His asthma has been
inflamed by the Vienna dust.

ALOYSIA:
I need you as my chaperone, Constanze.

CONSTANZE:
Chaperone? Every holy picture here is a chaperone. Even the
invisible Archbishop is a chaperone. Later, sister. Your servant, sir.

She curtsies and leaves. Mozart bows deeply.

MOZART:
Yours, madame, yours. Your sister has little of your beauty,
Aloysia.

Beauty, beauty, beauty.
I worship it still.
Your image in my brain
Impairs my will.

I tremble in your presence,
As them, no less.
I tremble at the essence
Of queenliness.

ALOYSIA (*soprano*):
You presume.
There's no room
In the house of song
Where I belong
For rash and rude
Boors to intrude.

MOZART (*kneeling*):
Beauty, beauty, beauty —
It vanquishes me.
It floods my aching eyes.
I only see
A scintillant aurora
Of light, of fire.
Oh yield to your adorer,
Admit desire.

ALOYSIA:
Go away.
Go and play
At amorous rage
Upon the stage.
You're indiscreet.
Get to your feet.

MOZART (*rising*):
Were I to write
Some brilliant bright
Confection of air
And earth and light

Only for you,
Then might I dare
To woo, to woo?

ALOYSIA:
You owl, you hoot,
If I may mute
Your wholly absurd
Nay mad pursuit
Of me, no less,
Why then the word
Might well be yes.

MOZART:
Yes to my wooing?

ALOYSIA:
Yes to your doing
What you said you'd do.

MOZART:
Music for you.

ALOYSIA:
Nothing improper — a
Wholly chaste opera.

MOZART:
Lucretia unravished,
And there will be lavished
Such wealth on the score of it
You'll cry out for more of it.
Agreed?

ALOYSIA:
Agreed.

BOTH:
Agreed. Agreed. Agreed.

Enthusiastically, he takes her hands and tries to whirl her around. To a loud chord the Prince Archbishop up center makes a dignified entrance, flanked by his Secretary and Majordomo. The Majordomo blows on a small trumpet and, to a march tune, the servants enter.

HIERONYMUS COLLEREDO (*tenor*):
Unseemly. Undignified. Learn your place.

SERVANTS (*led by Majordomo*):
Your place. Your place.
Humbly humbly humbly humbly
Learn your place.

MOZART:
Apologies, Your Highness and Grace.
We know each other. That was no embrace,
Merely the celebration of a pact.
I'll write an opera. She'll sing, she'll act.
Grant me the time to write it. On my knee
I beg you.

COLLEREDO:
You're indentured, sir, to me.

SERVANTS:
To him, to him. He is our lord,
Granter of life, of bed and board,
Just punishment and just reward.

COLLEREDO:
The hour of the Angelus.

He looks at his ornate watch. Promptly a bell tolls.

Madame, my gratitude.
And yet I can't approve this moral latitude.
You come without a chaperone.

Constanze runs in.

CONSTANZE:
Ah no,
Your Grace and Highness. Where she goes, I go.

COLLEREDO:
You graciously agreed to sing for us
Salieri's setting of the Angelus.
Sir, to the keyboard. You, the court musicians,
Take up your instruments. Assume positions.
Sing. Play.

SERVANTS:
Sing, play,
Play, sing.
Make our day
With some little thing.
Breathe, horn.
Strike string.
Set a bourne
To our suffering.

Mozart takes a manuscript from Constanze, who smiles in sympathy and attraction. A fortepiano is wheeled on. Mozart is torn between some doubt about the manuscript and some pleasure in the instrument. He strikes up part of a concerto. The orchestra follows him.

COLLEREDO:
Blasphemer! Blasphemer!
Your desecrate the hour.
Some foul demonic schemer
Has got you in his power,
Or else you're too moronic —
I rather think you are —
To separate the sonic
Sacred and secular.

SERVANTS:
The secular and sacred —
What do they signify?
He doesn't know the difference.
Neither do you or I.

Mozart and the orchestra play the opening of the Angelus. Mozart listens in growing horror.

ALOYSIA:
Angelus Domini nuntiavit Mariae . . .

MOZART:
To hell with angels? Hell with holy Mary!
This is no composition of Salieri.

COLLEREDO:
Take him away. Bar him with bolt and chain.
Not blasphemy, but softening of the brain.

MOZART:
This melody's
Not his.
The bastard, he
Stole it from me.

Mine, mine —
The thieving swine.
I'll get him, I will.
I'll rend, kill.

COLLEREDO:
Take him away, I say. There's madness in you.
We regret this, madame, but please continue.

MOZART:
I forbid it, I forbid.
This foul thing that he did
Merits a deeper hell
Than Mother Church can sell.
My inspiration is
Smeared with banalities.
This is a black offense
Admits no penitence.

COLLEREDO:
The truly black offense
Is your damned insolence.

SERVANTS:
Insolent scraper of gut,
Thinks he's our superior.
The case is open and shut.
Lambast his posterior.
Pardon us, ladies —
Send him to Hades.

CONSTANZE (*soprano*):
Forgive him, sir.
He has good reason.
To plagiarize
Is worse than treason.

ALOYSIA:
Don't give him, sir,
The chance to season
Such blatant lies
With spurious reason.

Observe the look	Observe the look
That films his eyes.	That films his eyes.
Administer	Administer
A brief rebuke.	A grand rebuke.
Make it appear	Out on his ear.
What happened here	He is a mere
Did not occur.	Ungrateful cur.
Forgive him, sir.	Dismiss him, sir.

MOZART (*who has attended only to Constanze's plea*):
Kind sisters, I don't need
The mercy that you plead.
The hour has struck
To venture low or high
And nevermore rely
On dubious luck.
You, sir, on you I spit.
Your morals match your wit,
And both your ear.
So Polyhymnia's curse
Strike you, or something worse.
I'm finished here.

COLLEREDO:
Finished is right, analphabetic lout.
You, Majordomo! Kick the dastard out!

The Majordomo advances to do this, but Mozart kicks him first. He beckons Lorenzo, who adds a kick of his own. Both leave while the entire assembly sings, all except Constanze.

ASSEMBLY:
O Mozart, damned and dead,
How will you earn your bread?
You leave this kind abode
To tread a lonely road.

Ungrateful, coarse and crude,
Blind to beatitude,
Imbibe a bitter brew.
We'll hear no more of you.

CURTAIN

*   *   *   *   *

ROSSINI:

Brief, I think. It has the feel of brevity. I will not judge the music till I know who the composer is. Barman, this champagne is insufficiently iced.

BARMAN:

Impossible, sir. Comrade, rather. Forgive the deference. I've only recently arrived. I'm not yet out of the habit of being servile. Anyway, it has to be cold enough. You're in a place, so they tell me, where all your desires are satisfied.

STENDHAL:

There is no real satisfaction in satisfaction. "The greater torment of love satisfied." Not a bad line. As for love, there seems to be nothing between the onset and the completion. Here, I mean. Perhaps we're really in hell.

ROSSINI:

Observe the queenly shoulders of that Russian princess, Henri Beyle. Observe her alabaster arms, the swell of her superb bosom. I can, I thank our great sustainer, view her aesthetically. That was always difficult in the former life. Lust always got in the way of the appreciation of beauty. And there is no greater beauty than a woman's beauty.

BERLIOZ:

A very large glass of Armagnac. I thank you. Gentlemen. A very trivial little opera. But we are all past the great passions.

STENDHAL:
More or less what I was lamenting.

BERLIOZ:
I had understood that there was no marriage in heaven. But poor little fat Harriet has been around, pestering me. She has left her Irish heaven to seek me out. She swears I swore eternal love. She says, and I cannot fault her logic, that as this is eternity, the vow holds. If only she would make herself as she was when she made all artistic Paris weep as Ophelia. But there is no reversion in heaven. We bring all our experience with us. Perhaps we're really in hell.

STENDHAL:
How strange. My sentiment word for word.

BERLIOZ:
Hide me. Shield me with your twin bulks. That is Harriet.

STENDHAL:
La Smithson?

BERLIOZ:
As was, before I dragged her into marriage, bad coffee, unpaid bills, lachrymose dipsomania. Ah, she's gone over to Rimbaud and Delacroix. They see only *la belle Ophélie,* icon of all our drownings. I don't. I gather we're here to celebrate the two hundredth earth year of Mozart's transfiguration. I see no sign of him.

ROSSINI:
He remains closeted with *der Alte,* as fat Goethe over there calls him. He's being kept in the dark about this offering. Its tone is ambiguous and possibly libelous. We don't want little Woferl rampaging all over the place. He has a foul mouth.

BERLIOZ:
Do the anonymous creators fear he'll bring them before the High Court of Heaven? I feel bitter about that undersized periwigged monster. More Armagnac, please.

ROSSINI:
Because he wrote better music than you?

BERLIOZ:
It's not better. There's just more of it. He started very early. Is music the only art that infects babbling infants — like thrush or chicken pox?

ROSSINI:
He finished early too. He didn't outstay his welcome. What would he have produced if he'd lived to my age? A hundred-and-fiftieth symphony with valve horns? No, he was done for when he died. He was lucky not to have to suffer a serene and sterile senility.

STENDHAL:
Did you suffer it?

ROSSINI:
I never took music too seriously. Except for *Guillaume Tell*. Seventeen ninety-one, that was the year he died. A kind of journalism. Sufficient unto the day is the *opera buffa* thereof.

BERLIOZ:
You too started early. I didn't. I had no infantile babbling period. I entered the art late and in desperate self-consciousness. I was probably not meant to be a musician.

STENDHAL:
A novelist, rather. Your *Symphonie Fantastique* is the best romantic novel we have — well, the best pre-Stendhalian. It is like

something by a man with a novelist's imagination but as yet no real grasp of words. So he takes a quick course in musical composition and tells his story in orchestral sound.

BERLIOZ:
Literature is the one true art. Music is merely there for its supererogatory adornment. Virgil, Shakespeare, Byron — I could not be them so I had to be their translator.

ROSSINI:
Their bookbinder, you mean. You gave them a superior sonic binding.

STENDHAL:
Rossini here was saying something about the separation of the biological urges from the aesthetic experience. He means the celestial condition, something predicated on a negativity, an absence. What is the difference between an angel and a saint? An angel never had a body, despite the winged angelographs of our childhood. Saints had bodies and retain the ghosts of bodily sensations. That is our situation. Swill that Armagnac from now till — I nearly said kingdom come — and you will suffer no headache or *gueule de bois*. Copulation is a cruel parody, for it ends only with the ghost of an orgasm. This should be the condition for the pure enjoyment of art, but literature is no longer to be enjoyed. We meet a heroine of great seductiveness, but we cannot be seduced. She and the hero couple, but we experience no erection of penis or even capillaries. Even without pornographical intent, the literature of physical love can mean nothing here. Therefore our great writers are relegated to an inferior circle of heaven. This is never admitted, but it is true. Music is the Armagnac of the saved. The musician alone has access to God.

ROSSINI:
God was always a fine intellectual concept, but it's his all too

physical son that inspired the loftiest music. My Stabat Mater, for instance.

BERLIOZ:
It's the words that move. The music merely seasons that meat of emotion. And, Henri Beyle, I wonder what you, a literary man, think you are doing here in this circle of the especially blessed.

STENDHAL:
I am an honorary musician by virtue of my adoration of our master here.

ROSSINI:
I'm touched. Always touched.

BERLIOZ:
What if literature evades the pull of the senses? I notice that Publius Vergilius Maro is admitted to what you term the higher circle.

STENDHAL:
As a magician, which is close to being a musician.

BERLIOZ:
I admit the music. I'm thinking of his phrase *flamma nota* for the sexual experience. Does that very unphysical summation free him from your attribution of the sensuous force of literature?

STENDAHL:
The phrase is the more erotic for relating to presumptions of sexual knowledge. The known flame, known so well that there's no need to describe it. No, music is the only art transferable to heaven. Or perhaps that horrible abstract painting that was found to be necessary when photography took over the recording of the actual. Architecture? Unnecessary and very physical. We have it chiefly because we have to have concerts and opera.

See how that cornice over there shivers with shame at its insubstantiality. But music is substantial in being insubstantial. There goes Beethoven, grumbling about something. He knows about that paradox, if anyone does.

BERLIOZ:
He's using an ear trumpet. But he does not hear the warning bell. We must go in. Barman, a very rapid Armagnac.

ROSSINI:
A very cold flute of brut.

STENDHAL:
Hector Berlioz, as a literary musician, you will perhaps appreciate the thing I have done. Here, where there is no worry about publishers, royalties, a scant readership, it is possible to practice the craft of fiction in a kind of musical purity. I have written something. Here it is — in print. It is brief, as you see. It is an attempt to write fiction in the shape of Mozart's Fortieth Symphony — the late one in G minor. Can one subdue human passion to musical form? Can one purge the emotions thereby? Read it. At your leisure. Or, if you're bored, during the performance of this next scene or act. I would welcome your opinion.

BERLIOZ:
It does not seem easy to read.

STENDHAL:
Meaning it is Stendhalian. Read it.

Act Two

SCENE I

The drawing room of the lodgings of the Webers in Vienna.

CONSTANZE:
The applause! It still rings in my ears. They loved you. And they
loved his music.

ALOYSIA:
It was very chaste. But there are some critics who accuse me of
insisting on a change in Roman history. Lucretia was ravished by
Tarquin.

CONSTANZE:
It was enough to have him attempt it and be stopped in time.

ALOYSIA:
It gives less force to my suicide aria. Perhaps the rape could proceed further than it did. The tearing of the garment, a passionate
kiss. That might be defilement enough.

CONSTANZE:
The music did enough ravishing.

Such genius, such skill.
The sounds are with me still.

The oboe's plaintive call,
Viola's rise and fall,
Acidic violin,
The drum and trumpets' din.
A living drama lit
The whole orchestra pit.
I could not keep my eyes off it.

ALOYSIA (*jealously*):
Sister, you should raise your optics higher.
Orchestras are fuel but not the fire.
They are the courtiers waiting on the queen.
Voices come from God, but violins
Are made with wood and glue and paint and pins,
And trumpets may be heard but seldom seen.

CONSTANZE:
It's true, there was a time
When voices were sublime
And wooden instruments
Humble accoutrements.
But now they have a soul
Which animates the whole.
They play a living part
In coloring your art
And striking to the inner heart.

ALOYSIA:	CONSTANZE:
Untrue, untrue.	It's true, it's true.
The voice is queen	The voice has been
Enthroned on high,	Enthroned on high
And song	Too long.
Will be as it has always been.	Now instruments invade the scene.
I'm right and you	I'm right and you
Are wrong.	Are wrong.

ALOYSIA:
Admire him, do you?

CONSTANZE:
Ah yes. Such fire, such originality.

ALOYSIA:
Such foul language, so filthy a wig, ragged stockings, bitten fingernails. If you want him, have him.

CONSTANZE:
It's you he adores.

ALOYSIA:
In vain. Yet I stick to the bargain. He wrote me an opera. Along with an equally foul-mouthed and down-at-heel librettist. My opera. My property. And in return he may woo. But not win.

CONSTANZE:
You're cruel.

ALOYSIA:
I shall not be so for long. Soon we start our German tour. He can't afford to follow me. And how can he seriously seek my hand when he has nothing in his pockets?

CONSTANZE:
He plays the fortepiano with some success. I went to hear him. He has pupils.

ALOYSIA:
They will not make him rich.

CONSTANZE:
You think too much of money. Of fine clothes. Of handsomeness and hypocritical good manners.

ALOYSIA:

One cannot think too much of money. Nor of the other things.

Elegance,
Opulence,
Cash in banks,
Cash in purses.
Deference,
Reverence,
Gracious thanks,
Graceful verses.
Silver forks,
Weekly baths.
Leafy walks,
Garden paths.
Bits of Latin,
Silk and satin,
Moderate health,
Immoderate wealth —
These
Please.

Poverty,
Penury,
Dirty paws,
Empty pockets.
Slovenly
Cookery,
Trademen's claws,
Pawnshop dockets.
Crusts of bread,
Heels of cheese,
In the bed
Frisking fleas.
Bitter quarrels,
Pauper's morals,

Harlot's feet
Upon the street —
Oh
No.

CONSTANZE:
That's explicit enough.

They start at the sound of a voice outside the window. It is Mozart with a mandolin.

MOZART (*off*):
The moon has risen, my love.
Her silver showers on me.
My heart's in prison. My love
Begs that you set it free.
You have the key.

ALOYSIA:
He expects an answer. He won't get it.

CONSTANZE:
This bold but bodiless voice
Belongs to none I know.
To you is given a choice:
Reveal yourself or go.
I wish it so.

ALOYSIA:
This is pure mischief. You are as good as telling him to climb up and enter. This is disgraceful. I will wake Father.

CONSTANZE:
Now's your chance to tell him face to face. Set him free. This is what he wishes.

ALOYSIA:
I would scratch you if I were not a lady. (*Leaning out the window*) Go. Go.

She tries to shut it, but Lorenzo is already on the window sill.

LORENZO:
You said he was to show himself. He will. I'm helping him up.

ALOYSIA:
I will not see him. I will fetch one who will beat you out of here with a big stick.

LORENZO:
Big sticks mean nothing to me, lady. My skin's pure leather.

Mozart appears. Both men are in the room. Aloysia flees.

MOZART:
She answered. Why does she run away?

CONSTANZE:
It was I who answered.

MOZART:
You?

CONSTANZE:
I. This has gone on too long.

She angled you, complaisant fish,
Till you acceded to her wish
And granted the vehicular
Device for making her a star.
Now your utility is spent.
She glitters in the firmament,

A vestal Venus burning bright
But only for her own delight.

MOZART:
This is untrue. It cannot be.

CONSTANZE:
It's all too true, as you will see.

MOZART:
If it is true, I'll take my score
And she'll not sing it anymore.
I sometimes feared that this might be
Although a lover's cecity
Approved my dangling on a rope
Whose strands were woven out of hope.
And now I reel in vertigo.
Oh, tell me that it is not so.

Aloysia comes in with her asthmatic father, who carries a stick.

ALOYSIA:	FATHER:
Here is the man,	Go.
Here are the men.	Go.
They will not bother	No?
Me again.	So —
His protestations	Out,
Make me sick.	Lout,
So *batti batti*	Lout,
With your stick.	Out.

He feebly beats the two men. The effort is too great, however.

MOZART AND LORENZO:
We've had quite enough of this
In archiepiscopal palaces.

The lordly shout, the loutish clout,
And so we justifiably flout
The violence of such as you,
A commoner, and senile too.

*The old man strikes Lorenzo, who cannot resist hitting back. The
asthmatic attack that follows fells the father.*

ALOYSIA AND
   CONSTANZE: FATHER:
I (she) should have thought   Back.
Before I (she) sought   Back.
Your aid.   Lack. Breath.
Oh Father dear,   I.
You're hurt and we're   Lie.
Afraid.   Near. Death.

*He struggles to his feet and his daughters lead him off. Mozart and
Lorenzo look at each other.*

MOZART:
Women are a frightful pest.
Not to fall for them is best.
Save one, perhaps, save one.
Now I'm loosed from passion's grip,
Seeking mere companionship
With one, perhaps, with one.

LORENZO:
I've courted and sported enough in my day,
Cavorted and snorted in passion's affray,
And swive them not wive them is all I can say.

MOZART:
Save one, perhaps, save one.

LORENZO:
I find no exception to shatter the rules.
The lesson you learn in the amorous schools
Is: those who seek bedding through wedding are fools.

MOZART:
Save one, perhaps, save one.

They depart the way they came. A double scream comes from the two sisters, off.

SCENE 2

A billiard room in the imperial palace. Mozart runs and runs the white ball up and down the table. Gluck is with him, very ill.

GLUCK:
I would offer you a game but, alas, I'm too feeble to hold a cue.

MOZART:
In billiards, in billiards,
I hear milliards of themes in the run of the ball.
Relaxing, relaxing,
There's no taxing of cerebral substance at all.
Monodic melodic
Rhapsodic imaginings come from without,
With shunning of cunning.
The running of balls is what music's about.

GLUCK:
I don't understand you.

MOZART:
I mean that music's as natural as the laws of physics. It comes.
Apples obey the behest of gravity. They fall. Music falls.

GLUCK:
To me it has always been a matter of hard cerebration. Composition is an intellectual process.

MOZART:
You worked in a highly intellectual city. With very good violins. You've heard my *Paris* Symphony?

GLUCK:
I don't see the connection. Paris is, to speak the truth, a very frivolous city. No opera without leg waving. And the young loud bloods arriving only in time for the ballet.

MOZART:
You find Vienna less frivolous?

GLUCK:
It granted me this imperial post. Which I trust you will assume after my resignation today. Court composer — a fine cachet. The salary is another thing. They forget to pay it.

Gluck coughs bitterly.

MOZART:
You are not well, Herr Gluck.

GLUCK:
I've reached the age of seventy-three —
Enough for any man.
A baffling ban
On being what I wished to be
Has blighted me.

The exiguous talent I possessed
I husbanded with care,
And used it where

It glimmered at its very best.
You know the rest.

With Calzabigi's aid
I made
The operatic stage
Engage
A truth it had not known.
Alone,
My sounds were brainless birds,
The words
The substance. They explain
My pain.

It is the poet who's the hand
That spins the mindless ball
Musicians call
Their art. Attain your dotage and
You'll understand.

MOZART:

Orfeo remains a triumph. And *Iphigénie en Tauride*. As for *Echo et Narcisse* — you must blame the Paris public.

GLUCK:

It is the public that kills or kindly permits to live. If Paris rejected my last opera, then Paris had to be right. But mark me well when I speak of operatic success. Your *Figaro* will survive because of its libretto. The triumph is Lorenzo da Ponte's. And Beaumarchais's.

MOZART:

Lorenzo has written words for Salieri. Will Salieri survive?

GLUCK:

A propos. Watch Salieri. He intrigues against you. You realize he is the other candidate for the post? And he does not have the scandal of *Figaro* to contend with.

MOZART:
There was no scandal in the music.

GLUCK:
Can you be sure of that? They are slow in making their choice. I wish they'd hurry and let me go home to bed.

MOZART:
The Emperor himself is engaged in the election?

GLUCK:
Very much so. Ah, we talk of angels and one wings his way towards us.

Salieri comes in, followed by a footman who bears a decanter and three glasses on a silver tray. He places this on a small table and, bowing, leaves.

SALIERI:
Gentlemen. Your wife is well, Mozart?

MOZART:
Constanze is blooming.

SALIERI:
I saw her on Berggasse. She looked dropsical.

MOZART:
What is termed advanced pregnancy, Salieri.

SALIERI:
Which enforces the denotation of her name.

MOZART:
Are you implying something?

SALIERI:
A mere pleasantry. *Così Fan Tutte* would make a good opera title. Gentlemen, I ordered wine, not, of course, for any *brindisi* of congratulations. The Emperor, I presume, will broach his somewhat acidulous champagne for that. A matter of beguiling the time of waiting. Permit me to pour. I think we may drink to something. What shall it be?

MOZART:
To the better man's winning.

GLUCK:
I will not drink to that. Who shall define what or who is better or worse? An imperial election is bound to have too much of the arbitrary in it. Let us drink to — oh, counterpoint.

SALIERI:
You pronounce the term sourly. Handel's words still rankle? About his cook knowing more of *contrapunto* than your esteemed monodic self?

GLUCK:
I never aspired to being a baroque weaving machine. But that was cruel, Salieri.

SALIERI:
Counterpoint is a cruel discipline. Let's drink to its cruelty.

THE THREE:
The cruelty of counterpoint,
The toothache of the fugal,
The twinge in each creative joint.

The public loves the frugal
Enjoyment of a bugle,
But we must slave at counterpoint.

At four- and five-part counterpoint,
The dovetail of the voices,
The midnight potions that anoint
The engine that rejoices
In stringency of choices,
The creaking wheels of counterpoint.

GLUCK:
My fugues were ash and rubble.

MOZART:
I never had much trouble.

SALIERI:
(And that's the bastard's trouble.
I'll prick the bastard's bubble.)

GLUCK:
The real or tonal answer —

MOZART:
Mere dances to a dancer.

SALIERI:
(I'll trip this flighty dancer.
God, let him die of cancer.)

THE THREE:
The mastery of counterpoint,
The mystery of counterpoint,
Subjection to its rules

Will make your rating mount a point
In the pedantic schools
Where analytic ghouls
Probe strictly at strict counterpoint
The strictest strictest counterpoint,
The fools.

MOZART:
Rules, as they say, are meant for breaking.

SALIERI:
Even rules of decorum and, I may say, loyalty?

MOZART:
What do you mean?

SALIERI:
I mean *Le Nozze di Figaro*. A feeble blow at the imperial hierarchy, but still a blow.

MOZART:
I prefer to consider it lighthearted rather than feeble. It gave no real offense.

SALIERI:
You seem not to have attained the kind of maturity capable of knowing what a real offense is. Do you consider yourself mature enough for this court appointment?

MOZART:
I'm only five years younger than you.

SALIERI:
I wasn't talking of age. The question of decorum is surely of some moment. You realize there are murmurs about your wife's behavior?

MOZART:

You mean that she goes forth alone while I'm engaged in strenuous composition? This is her right. Austria is not a colony of the Turks.

SALIERI:

Well, I suppose you must consider yourself entitled to your own view of marriage. Even to your view of courtship. Causing the death of your father-in-law-to-be was, I take it, an acceptable beginning.

MOZART:

This is all nonsense, Salieri. I know of the slanders you put about. Why don't you come out loud and bold and admit some more professional emotion?

SALIERI:

Such as?

MOZART:

A man who steals another man's music must have a reason for it.

SALIERI:

You call me a thief?

GLUCK:

Friends, friends, this will not do. His Imperial Majesty will be summoning one or other of you shortly. Be calm. Exercise restraint. Take another glass of wine in some semblance of amity.

SALIERI:

Very well. For you, Herr Gluck?

MOZART:

I did not start this.

GLUCK:
Thank you, no.

Salieri pours with his back to the others. He hands Mozart a filled glass.

MOZART:
That is a very Lucrezia Borgia ring you are wearing.

SALIERI:
Florentine, not Roman.

MOZART:
Let us exchange glasses, in token of the semblance of amity Herr Gluck urges.

SALIERI:
I don't drink from another's glass.

MOZART:
Or tankard, mug or demitasse.
Fearful of some infection?
Sir, I assure you, I could pass
A medical inspection.

SALIERI:
You're mad enough to have in mind
Poison, or something of the kind.

MOZART:
You spoke the word in question.
I sniff this goblet and I find
A source of indigestion.

SALIERI:
Fool.

MOZART:
Murderer and plagiarist.

GLUCK:
Come, gentlemen, I must insist
You exercise discretion.
It's most unseemly. Stop. Desist.

MOZART:
It's merely the expression
Of cordial trust and fellowship.
Come on, Salieri, take a sip.

SALIERI:
I drink to your perdition.

He drinks off his own wine.

MOZART:
Now press this other to your lip.
Kind sir — with your permission —

A tussle. It ends with the allegedly poisoned wine being thrown in Salieri's face. He tastes it and gasps. Gluck, in cardiac distress, falls into his chair. The door opens. The Emperor enters with his court. His Chamberlain announces him.

CHAMBERLAIN:
His Imperial Majesty Joseph II.

COURT:
Lèse-majesté, lèse-majesté —
Herr Gluck has failed to rise.
Salieri's in some disarray.
Can we believe our eyes?

Salieri, drenched and coughing dangerously, clumsily bows and runs off.

EMPEROR:
Our ancient *Kammermusicus*
Makes no obeisance to us.
It looks as if we are
Pushing reform too far.

And he we chose to take his place
Removes his sad and sodden face
In token of rejection
Of our proposed election.

These democratic manners show
That liberal change must go more slow.
The Empire only lives
Through firm prerogatives.

No matter now. Herr Gluck resigns.
Salieri, so it seems, declines.
Bereft of other choice,
We give Mozart our voice.

MOZART:
My thanks to Your Imperial Majesty.

Gluck's given up his post,
Also, it seems, the ghost.

COURT:
Dead! So Gluck is dead.
That more than Orphic head
Floats down the river, free
To join Eurydice.

EMPEROR:
Remove him. Fix his funeral
And fitting burial.

MOZART (*bitterly*):
So perish all composers, rich
Only in Orphic wine.
Drain it, and then assign
The bottle to a ditch.

The Chamberlain supervises the removal of Gluck's body. He then announces Mozart's appointment.

CHAMBERLAIN:
Johannes Chrysostomus Wolfgangus Theophilus Mozart is hereby appointed *Kammermusicus* at an annual stipend of eight hundred gulden.

MOZART:
Eight hundred! Gluck received two thousand!

COURT:
Gluck was Gluck. Mozart's Mozart.
Gluck produced eternal art.
Yours is a different circumstance.
You'll merely help the court to dance,
Provide a background for its chatter.
What does music really matter?

MOZART:
Cannabich at Mannheim earns eighteen hundred. Dittersdorf gets two thousand seven hundred. And what are they?

EMPEROR:
Learn decorum, sir. I may
Remove this honor right away.
It is not fitting to discuss
What a mere *Kammermusicus*
Receives from the imperial fisc.

In a less liberal day you'd risk
Your head and not a mild rebuke
From one prepared to overlook
Your lowly ignorance of the sort
Of manners proper to a court.

MOZART:
With all due deference, sire, I bow
And even grovel.
But is not Europe changing now?
In hut and hovel,
In German *Schloss* and French *château*
Sensitive noses
Scent something in the wind and know
It is not roses.
Rousseau, Voltaire and Beaumarchais
Have warned already.
The autocrats have had their day.
I hear the heady
And steady music of the march
Of common people
Ready to fell the imperial arch,
Tear down the steeple.
May not musicians join the throng,
At last respected,
The honored fonts of honest song,
No more dejected
As mere discardable machines
Wound up to tickle
The ears of emperors, kings, queens
Whose tastes are fickle?
I realize that what I say
Seems rank sedition,
But let me hail it while I may —
The coming dayspring of his day:
The free musician!

COURT:
Horror! Horror! Treasonous!
Thus a *Kammermusicus*
Risen from the ranker ranks
Speaks his thanks.

EMPEROR:
Freedom's ever relative.
Emperors are free to give.
You have freedom to refuse
And may choose.

Freedom to eat humble pie,
Freedom to decay and die,
Pen your bass or treble clef
For the deaf.

Write your music, hold your tongue.
You are young but not too young.
The gold mouth that's in your name
Learn to tame.

Freedom's ever relative.
I have freedom to forgive.
Freely I extend it. So
Let us go.

*To the imperial march the court leaves. The Chamberlain, who is
last, throws a sour look at Mozart, who bows deeply. The room is
left to him. Peevishly he bounces a ball on the billiard table. It gets
up and hits him.*

CURTAIN

*   *   *   *   *

SCHOENBERG:
Martinis, George?

GERSHWIN:
Like they say, a bottomless jug. And cold. Real cold.

SCHOENBERG:
This *opera buffa* is absurd. Travesty. Biographical falsification. Mozart's life was not like that.

GERSIIWIN:
What do you expect from a mere entertainment? The truth? The truth doesn't fit into a musical.

SCHOENBERG:
Any musical work, however humble, should be in the service of truth.

GERSHWIN:
Like *Moses and Aaron*?

SCHOENBERG:
Pass the jug. Myth can tell the truth. About human relationships. About power, God, virtue.

GERSHWIN:
Right. So the historical facts don't matter. But what the hell music has to do with any kind of truth beats me. Truth has to be in words. Your Moses tells the truth so he doesn't even have to sing —

SCHOENBERG:
He is slow of speech. I follow the Bible.

GERSHWIN:
And Aaron the liar and blasphemer is all music. It won't wash, my friend. Music is what it is. Keep truth out of it.

SCHOENBERG:

The truth is that there are twelve notes in the scale. No more, no less. Mozart speaks that truth at least once. Listen.

A pure tone-row with a few trimmings. The truth of what is in nature.

GERSHWIN:

The chromatic scale's not in nature and you know it. Or if it is, it's too high up the harmonic series to make sense except to a bat.

SCHOENBERG:

Your music is jazz or something like it. Picked out on a piano. You're not supposed to know about the harmonic series.

GERSHWIN:

Lennie Bernstein couldn't resist doing a replay of his Harvard lectures as soon as he got here. But Ravel had told me all about it in Paris that time. You should have dropped all that twelve-tone stuff as soon as you got to L.A. It didn't fit. All the studios wanted was straight tonic and dominant with a few fancy bits added. That's nature. That's truth.

SCHOENBERG:

Mozart's truth, meaning evasion of the truth, except when the light broke in for a measure or so. You know what tonic and dominant stand for?

GERSHWIN:

You told me before, Arnold. Stability. And it's okay to blue the stability with a few extra notes, like I did. But underneath the goo and tinsel you have the Torah or Bible reality. Nature says it. C is the boss but G is his deputy. They both wear badges. And so for the other law-abiding territories. C-sharp, G-sharp. D, A. E-flat, B-flat.

SCHOENBERG:

You needn't give me a kindergarten course on the key system. Listen. I spoke for democracy. Don't snicker, if that's the word. I denied hierarchy. I denied the structure of the Austro-Hungarian Empire, which was doomed. Didn't he die only two years after the first of the great revolutions? I said every note of the chromatic scale was equal to every other note. That was democracy.

GERSHWIN:

Sounding like anarchy. That's what Ravel said. He was a staunch tonic-and-dominant man.

SCHOENBERG:

He was French. He thought the center of cultural gravity was Paris. He was wrong. Everything that mattered happened in Vienna. Mozart and I look at each other from a distance, but it's only a time distance. We occupied the same space. What would anger me if it were worthwhile to be angry is the possibility that all I was doing was depicting the human unconscious. All right, sounding like chaos but deeply structured. All right, I was a contemporary of Dr. Freud.

GERSHWIN:

Your music's right and proper for the analyst's couch. That's what some of the studio music heads thought. But Hollywood

wasn't ready for Freud. Oh, I don't know. *Lady in the Dark.*
Kurt Weill wrote the score for that.

SCHOENBERG:
Another tonic-and-dominant man. One thing I do know is that
my music was never a depiction of heaven. Pass that bottomless
jug. Heaven's a hierarchy. None of us can be God. It was only
possible to have that aspiration on earth.

GERSHWIN:
You always worried too much. You thought of yourself as a mar-
tyr for the chromatic truth. But chromatic means colored. An
additive. The reality's black and white. Tonic and dominant.
Music was meant to entertain. Okay, it could slip in the mickey
finn of what you'd call truth when the listener was off his guard.
But Mozart had the right idea. His mickey finns are only about
the truth of himself, though. Here's your solid Viennese struc-
tures and, for the odd measure, here's me. Suffering. And as for
you, Arnold, you'd have rather written *An American in Paris*
than *Pierrot Lunaire.*

SCHOENBERG:
That work of yours is jazzily melodious enough, but it lacks
structure. No, I would have preferred to be Mendelssohn. But
I was destined to the martyrdom of the atonal pioneer. You were
destined to write tonic-and-dominant melodies and make
money.

GERSHWIN:
Destined also to die at thirty-eight. Older than Mozart, right,
but I had things to do. He hadn't. He'd done it all. I can still
smell those sharpened pencils. Aura, they called it. Brain tumor.

SCHOENBERG:
How far are we in control? What *Zeitgeist* was telling Strauss to

consider the destruction of tonality in *Salome* in 1905, me to start completing the job in 1912? What the hell was going on?

GERSHWIN:
It was the devil at work. The Mozart-killer. But we ought to be past asking questions about music. We *are* music. Let's go back in.

SCHOENBERG:
I've had enough. I will finish the unfinishable martinis.

GERSHWIN:
Tennis tomorrow?

SCHOENBERG:
If you let me win.

Act Three

Mozart's dwelling in the suburbs of Vienna. He is terminally ill, wrapped in shawls, seated in a not too easy chair, trying to work. But odd hallucinations distract him, as does his pain. He first sees and hears the dancers of a masked ball.

DANCERS:
Carnival, carnival —
It means farewell to meat.
Fish from Danube's foul canal
Is all we'll have to eat.
A Ramadan
More stringent than
The one that gripes the Mussulman
Will be tomorrow's treat.

Carnival, carnival —
There's flesh enough tonight,
Nectarous and ambrosial
And tempting us to bite.
So let's be rash
And cut a dash
Before the penitential ash
And curb on appetite.

Carnival, carnival —
Tonight the rules are rent.

For forty days and nights we shall
Have leisure to repent.
On Easter Day
We'll feast and slay
That beastly bristly bird of prey,
The holy ghost of Lent.

Mozart sees Lorenzo.

MOZART:
It's not Shrove Tuesday, is it? I can smell pancakes.

LORENZO:
You're nine months out. The kitchen's cold. The cook's gone.
I also would like some wages.

MOZART:
My wife has some money.

LORENZO:
The mistress has left too. She's in Baden.

MOZART:
I sent her ant's eggs for her constipation. Good for deafness,
they say. Also hairy cheeks on children. Did she try the bath of
cooked giblets?

LORENZO:
You can't afford that many chickens.

MOZART:
Where is Sigmund Barisani?

LORENZO:
Dr. Barisani? In purgatory, I should think. A great one for
purges.

MOZART:
Yes. Dead. And only twenty-nine. I've done better. There's no
hell, is there? We don't deserve hell.

LORENZO:
The way God treats his children here, I wouldn't put it past him.

MOZART:
No hell, no. No hell. That's certain.
The final curtain
Of *Don Giovanni* says there is.
Sheer fantasies.
Snakes. Demons. Stone *commendatore*.
A fairy story.
Better bed him down between
Pluto and Proserpine,
Nursing a lust he cannot slake
For Pluto stays awake.
The mason and illuminist
Have proved hell can't exist.
We confound hell in Elysium.
May that kingdom come.

LORENZO:
You're rambling, maestro.

MOZART:
Did you send for Dr. Barisani?

LORENZO:
Stone dead. Four years gone. As you know.

MOZART:
Poor Constanze. Pregnancy problems. She got a varicose ulcer
over little Anna Maria. Gout. Rheumatics. Glandular enlarge-

ments. Hemorrhoids. Uterine disorders. She ought to go to Baden.

LORENZO:
She's already there.

MOZART:
What do they say is the matter with me, Lorenzo?

Doctors in the guise of angels stand on either side of him.

DOCTORS:
Streptococcal throat infection,
Chronic inflammation.
Schönlein-Henoch syndrome
Adds a complication.
There's glomerulonephritis,
Hard pneumonic coughing.
We predict that renal failure
Is in the offing.
A mercurial overdose?
Quite out of the question.
Salieric poisoning?
An absurd suggestion.

MOZART:
Ave verum corpus. You know that piece of mine, Lorenzo?

LORENZO:
I never went in much for music of the higher sort.

MOZART:
Higher sort. Too Teutonic. Too difficult. Give us sweet Italian airs with a minimal accompaniment. Send the orchestra home. All we want is the singers. And how about the resurrection of the *verum corpus*?

LORENZO:
Corpses? A lot of that going on. Emperor's decree to cut down on cost of funerals. All paupers now. Common graves. No names. No ownership. Anybody's to dig up for the medical schools.

MOZART:
Ave verum corpus. It rots. A shitsack, Lorenzo. *Saccus stercoris.* I can't remember setting that. Got a letter from my mother. "*Addio, ben mio.* Stay healthy. I wish you good night. Stick your arse in your mouth. Shit up your bed till it bursts." Never a chance really, Lorenzo. *Madamina, il catalogo.*

Scarlet fever and catarrhs
At five. Rheumatic fever
At six. Typhoid, smallpox scars
At seven. A silver cleaver
Smashes dental abscesses.
Look at the young bastard: he's
Doubled up with colic,
Yellow with the jaundice too.
A holy diabolic
Something lets the music through.
Here is your Cartesian proof
That the spirit stands aloof.

Christ knows where it comes from, but it's not made of gray matter.

Constanze appears, not too solicitous.

She can't be here and in Baden, Lorenzo. Some little boy has been telling lies.

LORENZO:
Never said she was in Baden.

CONSTANZE:

I'd love to be in Baden,
Drinking salty waters,
Walking in the garden
With the Archbishop's daughters.

MOZART:

Stick your arse in your mouth, Constanze.

CONSTANZE:

Adultery's on the menu.
You eat it and imbibe it.
You choose your goat and then you
Succumb. The quacks prescribe it.

MOZART:

Shit up your bed till it bursts. Where, how and who are the
children?

CONSTANZE:

Hard to say really, Woferl. You know a mother's problems.
A father's too, I suppose. You were still writing that overture
while the audience was coming in. You couldn't attend to his
choking on a chicken bone.

MOZART:

Which child was that?

CONSTANZE:

One of the dead ones.

Death is rather a pretty thing
     When you come to think of it.
I buried my little puppy dog
     In a pretty little pit.

I covered it with summer flowers
  And sang a song and wept for hours.

Johann Nepomuk Hunczowsky
  Was hot for the baths at Baden.
I called my puppy Johann.
  I buried him in the garden.
Twelve sulphur baths all in a row.
  You really ought to go, you know.

  MOZART:

Rather busy just now, I'm afraid. Have to write this Requiem
and then die. Reversal of priorities really. Still, he paid for it
in advance. Wants to pass it off as his own. Fame, I suppose.
Has Franz Süssmayr finished copying the catalogue? Foresight.
What's mine is mine unless somebody else says it's his.

  SÜSSMAYR:

Johannes Chrysostomus Wolfgangus Theophilus
Mozart, sometimes Amadeus to us,
Though falsely, at the most was Amadée.
But Amadeus has proved an easy way
Of designating fabular Mozart,
Invented life matching inventive art —
The pauper's funeral man, the victim of
The venomous Salieri. How we love,
Better than art, these purple travesties —

  MOZART:
Get on with it, Franz.

  SÜSSMAYR:
Let us consider now his opuses,
Too much for one frail body. First there is
A tale of operas — here comes *Apollo*
Et Hyacinthus (at eleven). To follow

(At twelve) there's *Bastien et Bastienne,*
La Finta Semplice (thirteen) and then
Flows *Mitridate, Re di Ponto.* Now
Pubescent, let him take a manly bow
With *Ascanio in Alba.* In one year
Il Sogno di Scipione greets the ear
With *Lucio Silla.* Then a three-year pause.
La Finta Giardiniera gains applause
And, on its heels, welcome *Il Re Pastore.*
Zaide is a fragment. A true glory
Is this: *Idomeneo, Re di Creta.*
Observe the true skill of the stage creator.
And with *Die Entführung aus dem Serail*
His comic genius starts to raise a smile.

MOZART:
There was the thing that I wrote for Aloysia.

CONSTANZE:
No proof. Puchberg stole it.

SÜSSMAYR:
L'Oca del Cairo, Lo Sposo Deluso
(Both 1783) — these fail to do so.
Nor can *Der Schauspieldirektor* compare
With (1786) the fire and air
Of *Figaro.* He touches hell and heaven
With *Don Giovanni* (1787).
Così Fan Tutte, being somewhat cynical,
Fails to attain the operatic pinnacle —

MOZART:
Cut that. Cut it. The truest thing da Ponte ever wrote.

CONSTANZE:
That's hardly fair to me, Woferl.

SÜSSMAYR:
But with *Die Zauberflöte* godly breath
Afflates him, ready for untimely death,
And *Tito's Clemency*, the twentieth.

MOZART:
Impertinence. Signor Mozart is alive till he is not alive. What do
you mean, untimely? I am not a cooking egg.

SÜSSMAYR:
Now come the symphonies: 1 to 24
The non-Mozartian safely can ignore,
But hardly these — the 31st in D
(The *Paris*), *Haffner* (35, in same key),
The *Linz*, or Number 36, in C.
The Number 37 is nothing more
Than a slow prelude to an insipid score
By Michael Haydn. Proceed now to the *Prague*
(Or 38 in D). A *nouvelle vague*
Of inspiration rises and sustains
The three that follow. And so it remains
To laud the 39th (the key E-flat),
The melancholy 40th and that
Incomparable *Jupiter*. Ah, can it
Be judged less kingly than the kingly planet?
The choral works come next —

MOZART:
Enough, Franz. Or too much. Where did the money go?

CONSTANZE:
There was never much money. But there will be. Death's a great
enlivener of a man's work. Leave it to your loving widow.

MOZART:
Is it summer yet? Sing to me, Aloysia.

CONSTANZE:

Frau Lange is not available. She sulks. Not being foreign has ruined her career. Ruined yours too in a way. Music is by definition a foreign commodity. Our new Emperor has been too long in Tuscany. It's all Salieri and Righini for him.

MOZART:

Kicked out of his coronation at Frankfurt. Leopold. Like my father. No father to me. Sing, Aloysia.

ALOYSIA:

Summer has come to the Wienerwald,
   The foliage leaps with life.
And every husband is coralled
   With someone else's wife.
To die is hardly elegant
   Now summer's here to stay.
Reserve your quietal intent
   Till Advent's on its way.

MOZART:

So it's autumn now. The moon expands unconscionably. Pocked and fromatical. The swallows depart. Finish the Requiem, Franz. I scribbled a few sketches. Too many tonics and dominants. The stability of the Sanctus. I took the money, but where is the money? There's a ship sailing in. Its prow is shearing my frontal lobes. Is it already Advent? Christmas is coming.

LORENZO:

Three weeks off, maestro. You'll eat your goose cold. It's being fattened, just for you.

MOZART:

I did what had to be done. But gave them more than they asked for. Pretended the Empire's here to stay. But there's music to be

written. Inner convolutions. A picture of the brain. I dreamed
of a secondary seventh on the leading note of F-sharp major.
The upper note moved, transformed it into a French sixth. Then
the whole thing became its chromatic neighbor. Top note slid
up. Dominant seventh on E but no possibility of resolution on
the A triad.

CONSTANZE:
Delirious. Are you in pain, Woferl?

MOZART:
The head only. I mean, three white *touches* and three black
touches to follow. Why shouldn't it be a chord or a scale? Because it denies key, and key is the Empire. Very well, two keys
simultaneously. C-major arpeggio and F-sharp major arpeggio
played together. Excruciating but satisfying. A denial. Music has
to deny sometimes. Don't you agree, Papa?

HAYDN:
Prince Nicolaus is dead, dear boy,
   The Esterhazys undone,
So J. P. Salomon said, dear boy,
   That I should visit London.
Ah, you should see this ancient crock work:
I'm writing symphonies like clockwork.

The London weather's wet and shivery,
   But I have coal to burn.
Soon I'll be back in servile livery
   When the family return.
The conservation of the arts is
One of the tasks of the Esterhazys.

MOZART:
It won't do, Papa. We have to be free. Honest tradesmen selling
goods nobody wants. I kept my hair, see. No periwigged ser-

vitude now. I see great men shaking their massed and floating locks over resonant keyboards. Ah, my dear. The jeweled women swoon. The sexual ganglia vibrate with the triple strings. It will happen. Why is my right hand so cold?

COMMENDATORE:
You cannot loose your hand
    From this petrific grip.
Now welcome to the band
    Of the stone fellowship.
Music must imitate
The gestures of the state.

MOZART:
No! No! I'm free, I tell you.

COMMENDATORE:
The liberal intellect
    Bids chaos quickly come.
So stonily respect
    The stone imperium.
Giovanni knows this well
Now he is safe in hell.

MOZART:
There's no hell. We proved it at our lodge meetings. Rachbone. Not even this will last. I would give up music to breathe like an animal. Let me have air.

CONSTANZE:
The window is wide open, Woferl. See all those people coming in to pay their respects.

A JEW:
It was the stink of sweating nakedness that nauseated. And then there was no time for that luxury. The gas appeared, sinuous

angel of death. But at the moment of expiry I caught the strain.
A bar or so of the Quartet in B-flat. We praise thee that thy music did certify a heaven when hell began.

AN SS CAMP COMMANDANT:
The daily stench. One heaved over one's breakfast. It was not
fair to little Anna Maria. She vomited in the garden. Killing is
hard labor. But at the end of the laborious day of murder she
played the little Sonata in C and sent our souls skywards. We
praise thee that thy music did ease the strain of our pious duty.

A GERMAN STATESMAN:
We praise thee that thou didst testify to the world the Teutonic
gift of order.

CHORUS:
The wolves are ganging up.
The Baptist shares your cup,
The golden speaker too.
Love of the numen you
Exemplified, exemplified.
Your music never lied.

MOZART:
And you. And we. Hyacinths in some measure. An impossible
modulation. The ball goes cleanly into the pocket. There is
enough air. This is a rather suitable libretto. Sharpen a pen for
me, Constanze.

ALL:
A man must die, it seems,
    Before his life can start.
One of our major themes.

MOZART:
*Donne, vedete
Se l'ho in cuor.* ·

LORENZO:
In the polluted square
Polluted music streams.
   The maestro's grin is there.

MOZART:
Moreover, there is a certain . . . sourness . . . in the . . . combination of oboes . . . and horns. A matter of breath also . . . Breathe.

COLLEREDO:
Divines who load the shelf,
God is a Mozart air
   Discoursing to itself.

MOZART:
Is it . . . the development section . . . that depicts . . . human life? In which case . . . it is the recapitulation . . . that . . . cannot be . . . heard.

SALIERI:
He was no porcelain
Mantelpiece elf of Delf.
   There was a sort of brain.

MOZART:
Es ist genug. Tritone. On the mountain somewhere.

The curtain begins to fall.

CHORUS:
So nothing can remain
   And music is not sound.
Relationships retain
   The semblance of a ground.
   Abstractions spin us round.

CONSTANZE:
Now we have to begin.

CURTAIN

* * * * *

HENRY JAMES:
Totally preposterous. The travesty of the life of a great artist. Apart from the ineptitude of the execution, it is inadmissible to consider that the artist's personality possesses any pertinence to the artist's work. This is a heresy permeating the modern world. I met Robert Browning. He looked like a decaying stockbroker long steeped in philistinism. Where was the poet of *The Ring and the Book*?

DA PONTE:
What are you doing here? You are no musician.

JAMES:
Operas have been wrenched out of my work. Libretti ineptly fashioned. You are no more than a librettist.

DA PONTE:
The servant of a servant. Finally the servant of life. The work is only the discardable spume. Do you know Venice?

JAMES:
You should know that I know Venice. Once did she hold the glorious East in fee. The half-drowned palazzi. Cigarettes in the gondola. The delicious chants of the gondoliers.

DA PONTE:
You did not know Venice. You understood not one word of the *gondolieri*'s songs. Do you know Cenada?

JAMES:
Now, I understand, known as Vittorio Veneto.

DA PONTE:

My birthplace. A Jew whose father married a Catholic. Seminary. Latin, Greek, Hebrew. Ariosto, Tasso, Petrarch. They ravished me, but what were they for? To teach me how to dash off witty parodies. I attacked everything in the name of life. They threw me out of the seminary. An abbé, though, a man of the cloth. Have you heard of Carlo Gozzi?

JAMES:

I regret.

DA PONTE:

I learned from Gozzi. You can smell Gozzi in my libretti. The Accademia Granellesca. You know what *granelli* are?

JAMES:

I regret.

DA PONTE:

Cogliconi. Testicoli.

JAMES:

Really. I must execrate the vulgarity.

DA PONTE:

Meaning life. Venice was life. A total synthesis of the human. Excepting politics, but politics is not human. I could fulfill such religious duties as I had and at the same time swive like a rabbit. I lived in a brothel for a time, playing the fiddle for the customers. A brothel is the only shop where the customers do the serving. I wore my clerical habit. You are disgusted?

JAMES:

Faintly. I do not see what these revelations have to do with the separation of art from life.

DA PONTE:
If you want to understand *Così Fan Tutte* — and that you will admit is art — you must also understand the life that poured into it. And it is all accident. Art springs adventitiously from life. Listen. They threw me out of Venice for writing political sedition. I ran away to Austria. In Vienna I became poet to the Imperial Theater. Charm as well as talent. Poor Mozart lacked charm when he got past the infant prodigy stage.

JAMES:
He reserved charm to his music.

DA PONTE:
Salieri and Count Orsini-Rosenberg helped. What they called the Italian party. I got to the Emperor. I kept the post. Charm again. Of course, it was not all plain sailing. You see my teeth?

JAMES:
Teeth are a mere ornament here. Insubstantial. Incapable of biting. But I do not see why you should not conform to the aesthetic norm. Even Shakespeare has a fine full set. Your dentition is hellish.

DA PONTE:
A wound gained from love's lists. Nothing to be ashamed of. Rivalry. This girl loved me and a base Italian loved her. I had toothache and he gave me a curative ointment. It turned out to be nitric acid. Still, it is all life. Teeth or no teeth, Adriana Ferrarese fell for me even after her long liaison with Casanova. Casanova, of course, was my model for Don Giovanni.

JAMES:
Him, with some reluctance, I became acquainted with. The lady in question means nothing to me.

DA PONTE:

And so you shrug away from life. The girl from Ferrara grew up in Venice, and she brought the right Venetian spirit to Vienna. She sang. She sang Susanna in *Le Nozze di Figaro*. Mozart gave her new arias. He was as besotted as I was, but he gave up life for art. Well, for money. The art crept in. So much art was not really needed. You have never in your life known any woman like La Ferrarese. The sensual treasures, the capriciousness, the obduracy, the yielding. I sacrificed too much for her. No, can I say too much? Let me say *enough*. She was assailed by a thousand dreams of vanity and grandeur. Wealth was what she wished. I had to inform on her eventually. That was when I had been thrown out of Vienna. The chief of police, Count Pergen, was always after the Italian émigrés. I did nothing really. A few unwise words in the cafés, a seditious squib or two, an overbold letter in verse to the Emperor Leopold, not half the man that Joseph had been. He did not like me. Salieri let me down there, I think. Back in Venice I had to live. Informing on Adriana and her damned husband as disloyal to the state was a mode of ingratiation with the authorities. One has to do such things.

JAMES:

I am appalled.

DA PONTE:

Oh, you would be, with your pompous devotion to art. There is one thing I would be in accord with you. That Mozart's life is not worth presenting, since he neglected life for art. Your problem, I gather. The life of the composer of the three great operas is properly my life. The life of his music is a kind of abstract distillation of the life I put into the libretti. And their life was that of a man who dared. Have *you* dared?

JAMES:

There were certain difficulties. A bad back. A sexual orientation never clearly defined. There was little time for life, though some time for fictional exhortations to live it. It is the shape that the artist imposes on life that is, in a sense, the thing that life aspires to. The sweat, the intrigues, the teeth knocked out, the sexual diseases, the tears and occasional exaltations — we do not wish to know of these things. Mozart rises above them.

DA PONTE:
Rises above them, does he? He learned drama from me, and I learned drama from life. Life is an *opera buffa*. Leave tragedy to those whose ignorance of life bids them believe it exists. And don't imagine that you can draw Mozart into the imagined empyrean of some imaginary aristocrat who creates beauty while his servants do his living for him. There was not one thing that Mozart composed for which he did not receive a commission. I accept the division. Art versus life. But art only lives as bones live. Organisms decay, and life is organic. Heaven is no fulfillment. I pray to put on flesh again and return to Vienna. And Venice. And grasp that damnable Ferrarese in all her squirming nakedness. To hell with heaven.

JAMES:
Really.

K. 550 (1788)

First Movement

THE squarecut pattern of the carpet. Squarecut the carpet's pattern. Pattern the cut square carpet. Stretching from open door to windows. Soon, if not burned, ripped, merely purloined, as was all too likely, other feet would other feet would tread. He himself, he himself, he himself trod in the glum morning. From shut casement to open door and back, to and to and back. Wig fresh powdered, brocade unspotted, patch on cheek new pimple in decorum and decency hiding, stockings silk most lustrous, hands behind folded unfolded refolded as he trod to squarecut pattern's softness. Russet the hue, the hue russet. Past bust of Plato, of Aristotle bust, Thucydides, Xenophon. Foreign voices trapped in print (he himself, he himself read) and print in leather, behind glass new polished, ranged ranged ranged, the silent army spoke in silence of certain truths, of above all the truth of the eternal stasis. Stasis stasis stasis. The squarecut pattern of the carpet. He trod.

Towards window, casement, treading back observed (he himself he himself he himself did) ranged gardens, stasis, walk with poplars, secular elms elms, under grim sky. But suddenly sun broke, squeezed out brief lemon juice, confirmed stasis, a future founded on past stasis, asphodels seen by Xenophon, rhododendra of Thucydides. The mobs would not come, the gates would rest not submitting to mob's fury. He himself he himself he himself smiled.

Triumph of unassailable order. Versailles unassailable. Everything in its everybody in his place. Place. Place. Plate ranged
catching sun's silver. That other triumph then possible? But no,
what triumph in right assertion of right? Church rite, bed rite.
This much delayed. He himself he himself he himself did. Not
assert. Not assert. Not assert. Yet in moment when sun broke
salutary to assert. Hurt, no. Assert, yes. Brief hurt ineluct ineluct
ineluctable in assert, yet, in assert. Assert.

Out of door. Wide hall. Two powdered heads bow. Wide
stairs. High stairs. And yet (magic of right, of rite, of lawful assert?) no passage noted, he himself he himself he himself stands
by her door by her door by her door. Assert assert insert key. By
foul magic wrong key. Not his key. Yes, his key. But lock blocked.
Billet-doux spittled pulped thrust (not trust lust, though right,
rite) in lock, in lock? Anger hurled from sky? But no. Watery
sun smiles still.

SHE in room drinks off chocolate. She in bed still. Full sun
catches elegant body. Clothed but in satin sheets, in wool coverlet. In square fourposter lies. Note four for stasis, ages, gospels,
seasons. Four limbs stretched in lady's laziness. Two eyes meet
two eyes in silverbacked handmirror. Two breasts meet two
breasts in wallmirror as rises. As rises. She rises. Full day and
time for rising and day stretches. Long. She stretches. Long.
Two teethrows greet two teethrows in handmirror, wallmirror.
She own hair wears, brown, silk most lustrous. Bare feet on bear
rug tread. Not to be burned, ripped, merely purloined, no other
feet would other feet would tread.

Stubs toe on clawfoot (four, note four) of table marquetry.
Hurt, brief anger, who to blame? Subside, subside, pain. Pain
subsides. Sun rides. Not high. Day stretches. She stretches. Silk
the peignoir she dons, silver the comb she untangles tangles
withal. She is herself, content. He is himself, not so. Rite postponed, right unasserted. She combs.

Below in bright library he treads. Squarecut pattern of carpet.

Subdued his right. Rides her right. But what right? I rule bride, I rule by right. Land, harvest, harvesters. By right. Stretches in windowed sun. But back to glum morning (the squarecut pattern of the carpet, squarecut the carpet's pattern, pattern the cut square carpet. Stretching from open door to window). Repeat all. To here.

Not repeat. He himself he himself he himself treads. As sun retreats (not satin sheets, not wool coverlet), as son of sun king dreams, late abed, of cowering. He himself he himself he himself sneers, transferred to violent darkness, asserts and hurts. He burns, he rips, claims loins. Lionlike claims he. Nay, see him now split, into he himself and he himself. Appalled, he himself asserting stasis (Plato, Aristotle, Thucydides, Xenophon sct in busts' frigidity — who says fragility? What voice in xenophone shrieks frangibility?), the parterre and shaved lawn, the sempiternal elms set in sempiternal order, the rents in good gold pieces (gold is always the key, but we shift now from key to key, stasis gone under, silk rent for the better fraction), sees he himself himself transformed as lust thrusts out trust. Untrussed he lustfully lustily thrusts. Hot iron slaked. She herself not there but transformed to palpable scream beneath. Teeth grind, grip. Faces at windows peer in horror, in horror fists at doors knock. All shed, what no shed shredded. Of loins lawfully possessed. Stone lioness on parterre parturiates. He himself observing he himself appalled. The sun sackcloth hides shamed face in willed darkness. He thrusts and floods. Flood floods nether caves.

Not so. Not yet. Not ever yet.

The squarecut pattern of the carpet. Squarecut the carpet's pattern, russet, foxrusset. Stretching from window to door. Soon, if not burned, ripped, sheerly purloined, very likely, naked feet would filthy feet would tread. He himself he himself he himself trod in the chill wind that sang through the walls. From shut casement to open door and back, to and to and back. Wig powder like scant snow fallen, brocade rumpled, stockings silk now twisted, patch on cheek slipped, indecorous indecent comedone exposed, hands behind folded unfolded refolded, ring, a king's gift, off finger fallen lost in squarecut pattern's softness. Pat bust of Pluto, of Persephone bust, Charon in stone boat beckoning. Unforeign voices untrapped in print (he himself, he himself read, read the signs) and print in paper covers, behind glass now smeared, ranged ranged ranged, loud armies spoke of the untruth of the eternal stasis. Kinesis kinesis kinesis. The dissolving pattern of the carpet. He trod.

Towards window, casement, treading back observed (he himself he himself he himself did) ranged gardens, unranged, walk for the populus, secular laws laws under grinning sky. But suddenly sun broke, squeezed out brief lemon juice, confirmed stasis, a future founded on past stasis, asphodels most common flowers, rhododendrons trees of the dogrose. Would the mobs come, the gates submit to mob's fury? He himself he himself he himself scowled.

Triumph of unassailable order? Versailles unassailable? Nothing in its nobody in his place. Place. Place. Plate melted to mob money? That other triumph then possible? But no, what triumph in right performance of rite? In priestly hush. Sacerdotal solemnity. This much delayed. He himself he himself he himself did. Not assert. Not assert. Not assert. Sun did not break, insalutary to assert. Hurt, no. Assert, no.

Out of door. Wide hall in gloom. Two powdered heads bow. Wide stairs, high stairs. And yet (magic of right, of rite, by proposed tenderness conferred?) no passage noted, he himself he himself he himself stands by her door by her door by her door. By bright magic right key. Yes, his key. Lock not blocked. Momentary blessing from frail sun. Watery sun sadly smiles.

SHE in room drinks off chocolate. She in bed waits. Frail sun kisses elegant body. Clothed but in satin sheets, in wool coverlet. In square fourposter waits. Note four to be abandoned soon as eternal divisor. Two arms stretch, beckon in sad welcome. Two eyes meet two eyes in sad abandon. Silverbacked handmirror slides off satin floorwards. Two breasts with rosy nipples sadly greet. As rises. His rises. Full naked as sad time beckons, to frame in lethal steel the proffer of tenderness. She is his, he hers, they theirs, two are one. Lips sadly greet, sadly join. Wallmirror sees, indifferent as time's running. Her own hair, silk most lustrous, falls, silk, lustrous, odorous. Bare skin on bare skin slides, glides. Burn, lips. Loins conjoin.

Brief hurt, brief anger, what to blame? Nature, waiting goddess. Subside, subside, pain. Pain subsides. Pleasure rides. The silver light blesses. Day stretches. Both stretch. The sadness is of value unattained, now attained, devalued. The bright day will be done. Silk the peignoir she dons. She is herself, obscurely discontented. He is himself, now gone. Rite accomplished, right unacknowledged. She combs.

Below in dark library he treads. Squarecut pattern of carpet. The mysterious rite not refused. No talk of rights. I rule by right, however, and await the harvest. Stretches in windowed darkness. I drew her to myself, my darkness embraced hers. Time to envisage the coming time. They two, now one, confront chill winds. They themselves, they themselves, they themselves tread bare boards, uncarpeted, unrugged, and the polished planks disclosed as wormgnawed, and beneath them a darkness not of the coupling pair made one but of the disorder which strikes the assertive chords of a pretense of order.

Second Movement

THE black day is coming. *What black day is coming?* The black day is coming for you, me and everyone. *How soon now?* Quite soon now. The shadows closing, shadows closing. *I can see nothing.*

They are in a boat on the river in an afternoon of full summer. He rows, gently the oars dipping, rising, dripping. Idyllic, as they say. Overhead the boughs lean riverward lovingly, with such abundance of leaves that some may be given to the water between the green banks, green banknotes to be spent, not for spending. Finch, thrush, yellowhammer give out their notes more sparingly.

A black day soon coming. *What black day soon coming?* A black day soon coming. Engulf us everyone. *I'm happy.* Be happy. Our child grows healthily. The peaches are ripening on the wall. The harvesters are in the fields. The blue above is faultless. See the fish leap. She is in summer muslin, her wide summer hat laced under her chin. They row near to the bank that she may pluck a bunch of buttercups. *Do you like butter?* The buttercup glows onto her most delicate chin in answer.

They do not know butter. *They never see butter?* Bread without butter. And sometimes little bread. Husks, even sawdust. *How pretty those poor children on the bank.* Pretty if one takes in only their pallor, their huge eyes. Their bare legs are sticklike. *But I am happy.* I suppose we must be happy while we can. Soon I must row back. You are happy for your own reasons? *What do you mean? For your reasons too.* I think rather of him, you see. Who calls too often in the afternoons. Who bears gifts of newly published romances and brushes your fair bare arm with his sleeve. *He is harmless. And you are jealous.*

Perhaps so. Perhaps needlessly so.

The black day is coming. *What black day is coming?* The black day is coming for you, me and everyone. *How soon now?* Quite soon now. The shadows closing, shadows closing. *I can see something.*

You can see something who before could see nothing. How nothing stays still. How even this perfect day must end. And that blue above promises to be no longer faultless. There is a dead fish, see, floating belly up. *How horrid.* You believe love dies. But it does not die. It gains in depth what it loses in intensity. *You do not then love me as intensely as you did?* You are mine, queen of my small kingdom. Mother of my child. *You say that word "my" too often. My castle, my horses, my dogs, my library.*

You are welcome to all, especially the library. There are romances there, too. I will row back.

On the river in the late afternoon of, yes, fading summer. He rows, less gently the oars dipping, rising, dripping. A somewhat chilled idyll, as they say. Overhead the boughs lean riverward not lovingly, for they cannot love, with such abundance of leaves that some may be carelessly spent on the careless river. Yellowhammer, thrush, finch, blackbird give out spare notes. We're near now. *Near now. Near now. Nearing it now.* Echo answers. *What is that thing floating?*

A body. No, a head. Severed. (His reading has corrupted him. He thinks of the head of Orpheus. The mouth is open, but there is no song.) Do not look. No, I am mistaken. No head. A bundle of sedge floating. (It was a head.) *You said it was a head. How horrid.* I am sorry I said that. One does not see human heads floating down rivers. This is not a barbarous land. In the jungles I read of, in the countries of the headhunters and the eaters of flesh. *You eat my flesh.* Hail true body. The body of the Lord is eaten but ever renewed. So yours. Inner language of carnal desire confused with brute appetite. First law confounded with second. Of life. I have read the philosophers. In the library where the romances also are. We arrive. Boatman bowing boat tethers. The leafy path. The spaniels leap in joy.

I'm happy. You're happy. *So happy.* The black day is coming. *What black day is coming?* The black day is coming for you, me and everyone. *How soon now?* Quite soon now. The skies proclaim it. *Skies proclaim it?* Black, bleak and bitter. The blue night's arrived now. The blue night is with us. How urgent sighs the wind. So listen. *I listen.* The candles flicker, fleck the shadows. *We eat.* Some do not. *We eat.* So we eat.

Third Movement

THEY ply their instruments too swiftly. They play this minuet so sadly. The sadness is built into the music. They play fast because our leisure is eroded. The last ball a sad ball. The dancers, our guests, dance in unwilled agitation. The candles erode the shadows of the ballroom. But there are enough shadows.

She smiles and damps her smile too swiftly. He smiles and holds the smile too sadly. The sadness is a gift of the music? They play fast because their leisure is eroded? The last kiss a sad kiss. The dancers, our guests, dance in unskilled animation. The candles erode the shadows of the future. But there are enough shadows.

There's a kind of joy in it. The pleasure of the bad tooth bitten. The pleasure of the sour fruit eaten. No pleasure without pain, pain without pleasure. But my teeth are sound. Face in the danced-past mirror unsour. "Sour" not the right word. There is more than sourness coming.

And on a sour cadence the dance intermits.

He sees them seated in the shadows. *Stretti stretti,* as that song in Venice had it. *So happy* in the gondola. His arm is about her, but tentatively, tentatively. He fears me? There is nothing to fear. There are far greater fears to engage.

They do not see me seeing them seated in the shadows. *Stretti stretti,* as that song in Florence had it. *So happy* on the Arno. Her hand is upon his, but tentatively, tentatively. She fears me? There is nothing to fear. There are far greater fears to engage.

The kiss they exchange is but a butterfly touch of the lips. Farewell, no, not that. Not brotherly, sisterly. A token of promise? A token reminder of past passion? They do not move me to any traditional response.

The kiss they exchange is the dust of dead butterflies on cowslips. Farewell to flesh. Probe the final mystery. No rational premise. Faith the remainder of dissolution? I am not moved to any traditional response.

We accept that they play too swiftly. That they discourse this dance too sadly. The sadness is the soul of the music. They play fast because our insouciance is eroded. The last kiss a sad kiss. The dancers, our guests, dance in unfulfilled trepidation. The candles erode the shadows of the future. But there are enough shadows.

There is no joy in it. We are bad teeth for the toothdrawer. We are rotten fruit, yet to be eaten, no, spat out halftasted. The times are unsound. We see our faces in a sour mirror, the regime. "Sour" not the right word. There is more than sourness arriving.

But on a sour cadence the dance ends.

Fourth Movement

WELL, the tumbrils are coming. The word suggests tumbling, rumbling, thunder. Yet a tumbril is only a farm cart. Loud cry the crowds, cry loud the crowds, the crowds cry loud. Yet disciplined. Yes, disciplined. Discipline of the fullfed not averse to the serving of the daily feast. No longer hungry but will eat. Hungry no longer but will to eat still. Hunger and anger, neither any longer strangers. Disciplined. Anger of a people the steel of its soldiers. They cry out, out they cry, but the outcry is ordered. What will come will come, so welcome what will come.

And she is safe. Her winsomeness appealed, a peal of silver bells her winsomeness. The sun beamed on her release. On the dirty window behind her light fractured, her hair was caught in the web of the spectrum. A mother bereft, her our son trampled when the unthinking mob broke. Innocent rage from Eden fresh trampling the Edenic innocent. She did not plead, made no plea for me, for her. Indifferent.

Yet the release with no gentleness was accomplished. Your bright brown hair will blow in a free wind. Tug its brownness, brightness. Go, lady. In laughter. Bad teeth but not for the toothdrawer. We will draw your teeth. Then she no more.

Well, the gumbrills are humming. The birds ingest rumbling, crumbling, blunder. Yet a thumbril is lonely, a warm start. Loud crowd the lies, lies loud for the crowd, the crowds lie loud. Yet disciplined. No, we discipline. Discipline of the soon dead, the perverse serving of the daily feast. Feed the hungry. Give drink to the thirsty. The general will to eat still. Stranger and stronger, no longer a stranger the stoic discipline. Anger of a people the steel of its soldiers. They cry out, out they cry, in outcry disordered. What will come will come, so welcome what will come.

And she is safe. Her winsomeness won the bells to pealing out in consonance. Her son beamed on her release. On the dirty window before her light fractured, her hair was caught in the flow and ebb of the spectrum. A mother unbereft, her our son untrampled when the unshrinking mob spoke. Innocent rage from Eden untrampling the recognized innocent. Part of pleas, yet made no plea for me, indifferent. Bells break out in spectrum for the year One. For it is the year One. Hear the busy feet on the street confirm that it is the year One.

The tumbrils in frail consonance break. Time disordered, space in disarray. Idiot tongues fracture syntax. Unreason appeals to reason, and reason is revealed as unreason.

But treason rhymes with it. My reading is jumbled. My mastery of the syllogism of no account. The one truth: we will believe what we wish to believe. So will is primal and all else disguise. And the general will? It is no aggregate of individual wills. It is a cosmic substance muscled in its cecity. No use to say this here or there. The philosophers leer, secure, triumphant in their having in elegance and eloquence and the appearance of syllogistic rigor disguised the ravening will. This means nothing to them either here or there. Will will work its will.

AND so it will, with the tumbrils coming. Word suggests tumbling, thundering, thrumbling. The trussed geese on the farm cart. Loud cry the visible crowds, cry loud, spit too, spit wet and cry loud the crowds. The discipline in the heavens is not that of a theological system but of the birds indifferent to all this, disciplined in the immemorial cycle of feeding and begetting they do not understand. Hungry and will eat. Disciplined. Anger of a people confined by the steel of its soldiers. They cry out, out they cry, but the disordered outcry submits to order. What will come is coming, but welcome only the blackness after.

So she is not safe. She appealed with her winsomeness, a peal of silver bells the voice of her winsomeness. No sun beamed on her release. On the dirty window behind her life fractured in prospect, her hair strings for the diabolic plectrum. A mother bereft? Rather a son. Pleading, but not for me. She had time to prepare for the black time coming. The panic of her plea truly not forgiven. Two cells unlocked with the one key. And now this.

Better out of it. Regret? Ah yes, but one may not defy the general will, the cosmic ravening substance that, given time, will eat all. All consumed, all. A brave face on it under the people's steel. So be it.

* * * * *

ANTHONY:
Gibberish.

BURGESS:
Yes, a good deal of it. There's a musical structure underneath, filched from Mozart, but one art cannot do the work of another. Music is all verbs. Well, there are occasionally nouns, as in the opening of the Overture to *The Magic Flute.* There are phones but no phonemes. That gibberish is part of my program of evasion.

ANTHONY:
So you admit the evasion.

BURGESS:
Of course. I set up an improbable heaven with squabbling sanctified musicians in it, but Mozart is not among them. He is

talked of a little, just as we who are not theologians talk of God a little. But, two hundred years after his death, there seems nothing to say except how divine he is. He produced God's music. This, naturally, is nonsense. That he was a great musician we can have no doubt. If you want to discuss his great achievement we have to get down to the works themselves. I'm prepared to analyze them — well, some of them (he wrote far too much) — but analysis is for the musicologists, and here our concern is to justify the layman's adoration. This can be done only through evasion. We may talk of the man, but what is the relevance of the man to the composer? The puppet Mozart I set up in the stupid little *opera buffa* libretto I contrived will do as well as any travesty. If you want the man, that is. But the music should be enough.

ANTHONY:

A man wrote the music, not a disembodied spirit. He ran out of music manuscript paper and had to run out in the rain to buy more. Then he found himself without ready cash. He spilt the ink and found his quill badly cut. He had headaches and indigestion. He slept with his wife, and perhaps the rhythms of coition begot new themes.

BURGESS:

Irrelevant, all of it. We have the music, and the music is, if you will, divine. Why pry into the banalities of the suffering or exulting life from which it came?

ANTHONY:

We would prefer to discover a laundry list of Shakespeare's than the lost play *Love's Labour's Won.*

BURGESS:

We've heard all this before, and I would still talk of impertinence. Though I might concede that there is less of it when you confront a great manipulator of words. For words deal with real things, and to some extent we handle with the poet's words the things he held between his palms. That Shakespeare hated both spaniels and candy seems certain, and he hated spaniels chewing candy most of all. Edmunds and Richards in his plays are far from admirable, and he had brothers of those names. But we always end up with an aesthetic object which, if it can be considered in human terms, fails if those terms are not of the most general kind. But I doubt if music can be considered in human terms at all.

ANTHONY:
It's created by human beings.

BURGESS:
It has no referents. Meaning it doesn't refer to any known and definable human experience. It's not *about* anything. Attach words to it, true, and things change. But then the music recedes into the situation of a mere servant. Discuss Mozart's operas and we discuss how aptly he colors the words of da Ponte.

ANTHONY:
What then do we discuss?

BURGESS:
We don't discuss as much as clarify our own attitudes. For instance, we're all somewhat bemused by Mozart's precocity. Infant prodigies always overawe us. We become Wordsworthian and burble about clouds of glory and heavenly music almost emerging straight from the eternal world from which the prodigy has only recently been released. Yet Mozart's prepubescent compositions aren't all that remarkable. Very clever for a mere infant, yes, but nothing's revealed in them except a precocious talent for imitating his elders and betters. Nothing interesting emerges till after puberty's well set in. If Mozart and Mendelssohn had died at eighteen, there's no doubt who would be considered the better composer. Mendelssohn produced the

Midsummer Night's Dream Overture at seventeen. He never wrote anything better, and he knew it. That music can be produced so early in life, and that music can be performed more than adequately in babbling infancy ought to make us wonder how genuinely human it is. I mean, a child's not strictly human. He hasn't had the experiences out of which literature is made. We don't take six-year-old poetlings seriously, but some of us are prepared to listen with rapture to some little angel-demon rattling off his own banal little sonatina. There's danger in music.

ANTHONY:

Oh, I don't think anyone denies the danger. The danger of being moved by sheer sound, of experiencing a tremor of the nerves when the overtones of a trumpet ring out. Play a solitary chord of C major and you say: "How beautiful." Doesn't Samuel Butler's Miss Skinner say: "Give me a simple chord of Beethoven. That is happiness"? Danger in sounds that soothe, stir. Saint Augustine saw the danger, so did Sigmund Freud. Too close to the id, Freud said — whatever that meant.

BURGESS:

It meant too close to the irrational. We're defined as human entities by being capable of reason. And this adoration of the child Mozart is irrational. And yet if we revere the mature Mozart it's in terms of reason, or at least in terms of an epoch that we call the Age of Reason. His music is reasonable music, obeying rational laws.

ANTHONY:

You can't talk of music in such terms. Music is essentially an emotional experience. It makes one feel, not think.

BURGESS:

True, if it doesn't move, it's nothing. And yet it must, at its most authentic, make an intellectual appeal.

ANTHONY:

The intellect is concerned with ideas. There are no ideas in music.

BURGESS:

But what is an idea? A constraint on emotion. A formulation, a formalization, a form. The intellectual element in music is its form. Rhapsodize without form and you admit nothing but pure, or impure, emotion. Rhapsodies are often national — Hungarian, Spanish, even Welsh. No intellectual constraint on the welling up of patriotism, direct or referred.

ANTHONY:

Even a piece of rhapsodic music has form. A beginning, a middle, an end.

BURGESS:

Not enough. The greatest epoch of music took form further. Fugue, passacaglia. Eventually sonata form. The composer's complete submission to a prescribed pattern. That pattern was the sonic equivalent of the society which music served. The Age of Reason was the Age of the City. Society was urban. Outside lay nature, to be controlled if possible, ignored if not. Rhapsodic nature. The music of Mozart expresses belief in reason's greatest creation, the town. He submitted not only to the larger forms — symphony and concerto — but to the twigs and branches of the man-made tree. A matter of cadences, tags, minute formulae, chord sequences. He never broke out of the molds. He knew too that society, expressed spatially in urbifaction, in architecture, public statues, fountains, piazzas, was expressed temporally in the march and the dance. The march is the straight line, aggressive or protective. The dance is circular. The circle is the movement of mating, of renewal. Men and women, moving in a circular pattern, urged on by music, symbolized an eternal recurrence. Mozart knew all about this.

ANTHONY:

So did his contemporaries, most of whom we've forgotten. Why did he survive?

BURGESS:

A greater efficiency, a larger fecundity, the sly capacity to inflect.

ANTHONY:

What on earth do you mean?

BURGESS:

He supplies his own individual touch to the forms, seems to be about to distort in the service of self-expression, then draws back in time. The romantic instinct is there, but it's not merely controlled, it's quelled.

ANTHONY:

Romantic. Baroque. Rococo. Do these terms mean anything?

BURGESS:

In music, perhaps less than the specialist historians think. Baroque is primarily architecture, sculpture, painting. Ingenious extravagance, hitting the viewer in the eyes. The blinding magnificence of the Lord God, hence of his Church. It was a propagandist response to the Reformation. If we take Protestantism to be cleaned-up Christianity, then the Counter-Reformation replied that it didn't need cleaning up, it needed more overlays of color and exaggeration. God was not for the plain meetinghouse, where everybody sniveled with a cold; God was so incredible an entity that he had to be symbolized in incredible art. But inevitably this produced incredible artists glorying in incredible skills. Secularization on a large scale. Look at those impossible musculatures in the Piazza Navona in Rome. Bernini, so skilled in exaggeration that the baroque is always in danger of becoming the absurd. And how can music be baroque? I listen to a recorder sonata by Handel and I hear plenty of restraint, plenty of classical coolness, and yet I'm asked to call the music baroque. Undoubtedly the element of show-off exaggeration lay in what's not survived in the printed music. The improvised ornamentation on a plain enough ground. With Johann Sebastian Bach I find the term baroque making some sense. The intellectual extravagance of *The Art of Fugue*. To compose a five-part fugue is like carving a Bernini statue. Instruments do what they should not be doing — imitating the human voice, glorifying the essential human. The ingenuity isn't wholly cerebral, however. Stravinsky said you could smell the resin on Bach's strings, taste the reeds of his oboes. Mozart clearly isn't baroque, but he could imitate the baroque when he wished, just as he could push forward into the twentieth century in the *Dissonance* Quartet. The sons of the great baroque man, Karl Philipp Emanuel and Johann Christian, turned, following the Oedipal pattern, against the father. No more fugues, or not many. The invention of sonata form. The young Mozart drank at Johann Christian Bach's fountain.

ANTHONY:
Rococo.

BURGESS:
So they say. Rococo was a form of architectural decoration that came after baroque and deplored its excesses. Little curves in delicate networks, the relief very light, the colors white and gold. Early eighteenth-century French. The French liked wood, the Germans and Austrians stucco. Watteau is the great rococo painter, isn't he? Fantasy, but not the heavy eye-hitting, body-slamming dreams or nightmares of the baroque. Lightness, delicacy. Look at a Watteau and you hear Mozart.

ANTHONY:
Unfair to Mozart.

BURGESS:

As unfair to him as to Haydn. Or to early Beethoven. The big practitioners can't be limited by glib classifications. It's hard to put Beethoven into any of the easy categories.

ANTHONY:

Romantic.

BURGESS:

Prepared to be. Prepared to look at the world as well as the city, whose narrow proprieties he inflects with gross little jokes. Byron goes into the mountains, despising the city — that's romanticism, especially when he identifies himself with the mountains as towering, free, lonely, as assertive nature. In the *Pastoral* Symphony Beethoven sits by a brook and listens to birdsong. But it's not romantic, it's only a brief holiday from the city. The self doesn't overflow and absorb its subject. Even those naïve little bird chirps are confined within rococo pattern, encaged for the delectation of town dwellers. He's prepared, in the late quartets, to relinquish the set forms. Already long deaf, he now blinds himself to the constraints of society. But in the big public works he prefers to expand the given forms rather than shatter them. Take the first movement of the *Eroica.* It's immensely long and its coda is no longer the sweet little tail of the animal — it's almost a new and intricate musical argument based on the truth that C-sharp and D-flat both are and are not the same note. Mozart could have lived to hear it and he would have been in no more than early middle age. When was the *Eroica?* 1803? Mozart would have recognized regular sonata form and perhaps seen that his own concision fitted only an age that didn't like these damned musician flunkies to go on too long. Beethoven asserts personality in the new way — romantic, if you like — and says: I'm serious, so you'd better damned well listen.

ANTHONY:

The fewer the constraints, the greater the artist. It's the constraints that Mozart labors under which diminish him. Beethoven is undoubtedly the greater of the two.

BURGESS:

The more Napoleonic, if you like. But it was precisely the intrusion of the nonmusical that damaged him. He considered the *Eroica* his greatest symphony. But it's not pure music, as Mozart's symphonies are. Can we listen to the *Eroica* without imposing if not the image of Bonaparte at least the wraith of some colossal conqueror? Here's his funeral march and there he is transformed into Prometheus. Beethoven's paving the way for the symphonic poem. We can't listen to Strauss's *Till Eulenspiegels* or *Don Quixote* without consulting a program note that tells us which part of the music illustrates what part of the story. As for constraint, can we make a distinction between what's imposed by outer conventions and what the composer freely chooses himself? Schoenberg accepts terrible constraints, those of serialism. The artist cries out for freedom but knows that he can't accept too much. Freedom can be anarchy. Anarchic art is an impossibility. Mozart wasn't forced into the cage; he entered it voluntarily. Of course, he shook it a little, but he didn't try to get out.

ANTHONY:

Does his superiority to most of his contemporaries reside in his occasional shaking of the bars?

BURGESS:

You can put it that way. You can also speak of memorability, the capacity to shoot a straight arrow into the future. You can remember the themes of his work. There's the idiosyncratic touch, despite the conventional cadences. The bowing and scraping conformists, churning out sonatas and operas for a living, never bequeathed anything memorable to posterity. Except by some exceptional stroke of luck. Who remembers anything of Boccherini except that damned little, sweet little minuet?

ANTHONY:

In other words, Mozart had the melodic gift. As much as Haydn.
More than Beethoven. And here's the heart of the mystery, I'd
say. Bernard Shaw said that any fool could develop a theme. He
even suggested that there ought to be a bureau where would-be
symphonists could buy their development sections ready-made.
Creating a melody in the first place is the trouble.

BURGESS:

Don't confuse theme and melody. A theme by its very nature *has*
to be developed. A melody is complete and perfect in itself. Beethoven was better at themes than melodies. Take the opening of
the Fifth Symphony, fate knocking at the door or the call of the
yellowhammer or whatever it's stupidly supposed to be. Da da
da DA. It's developed into fragmentary melodies which are part
of a bigger pattern. A theme may have a beginning, but it has a
number of possible endings. Or no ending at all. Whistle a
theme and you soon tail off. A melody has a final cadence. Put it
into a large structure like a symphony and, as Constant Lambert
said, you can do nothing with it except play it again, this time
rather louder. Mozart had the thematic gift on a smaller scale
than Beethoven, but he had the melodic gift on a much larger.
Can you remember any melody from Beethoven's opera *Fidelio*?
Mozart's operas yield scores of perfectly formed melodic struc-
tures. Heartbreakingly moving, most of them, chiefly because so
restrained, so civilized.

ANTHONY:

You speak of a melodic structure. That sounds as if melodies are
hammered together, consciously and deliberately. Surely melodies must come unbidden. There's a large mystery in them.

BURGESS:

The hammering together was Beethoven's way. Consult his note-
books. He strained for his melodies. Costively, if you like.

Schubert, the greatest melodist of them all, found them in the air or springing out of the refined speech we call poetry. Mozart plucked them like fruit. I don't deny the mystery. Much of my life has been spent in wondering why one melody should be better than another. Technical analysis doesn't help. And the melodic hierarchy cuts clean across the accepted, traditionally snobbish, categories. I mean that Jerome Kern and the musically illiterate Irving Berlin produced better melodies than Wagner. If you can still be moved by "They Didn't Believe Me" seventy-odd years after it was composed, you're right to bring out the garlands. Mozart can compete with the melodists of whatever depth of brow. But we hear melodies these days with a frightful nostalgia. The melodic age is over, perhaps never to return. The serious composers work at what Aldous Huxley called an atomic level — submelodic, if you like. And the popular composers, if you can call them that, meaning the purveyors of rock, bang out a perverted heartbeat with a kind of banal recitative at the top. You can say that the death of melody at the serious level began with serialism. If the making of a theme, termed a tone row, con- sisted in the conscious arrangement of the twelve notes of the chromatic scale into a pattern for variations of a very restrictive kind — well, the free flower of instinct had been crumbled. Per- haps also our nostalgia has some guilt in it. Schoenberg said that the diatonic scale, no matter how thoroughly Wagner inflected it with chromatic flavorings, was already past its usefulness as early as 1865, the year of *Tristan and Isolde*. It had to yield to the chromatic scale. We feel in some ways that he was right, though probably for reasons he was unwilling to formulate.

ANTHONY:
Nonmusical reasons?

BURGESS:
No matter how rigorous the fundamental structure of an atonal serial work, the ear and brain have the impression that this is the

music of, yes, social breakdown. So we feel guilty in returning to the music of Mozart, in which the integrity of society seems to be symbolized. We feel guilty about the diatonic scale, the plain, confident do re mi of an age of assurance. We feel guilty about accepting the Schoenbergian postulate with our minds but rejecting it with our hearts and senses. We feel at home with Mozart and then suddenly realize that we're not dressed for pre-revolutionary Europe. We're putting on an act.

ANTHONY:
You see, you can't keep nonmusical considerations out of all your fine talk of Mozart's pure music. I think you might accept that we can't understand Mozart unless we understand the period that produced him, and that means understanding an exceptional product of the period, though one thoroughly at home in it. We have to know something about the man.

BURGESS:
I concede that we'll know more about why he wrote as he did if we consider Mozart as a working musician. You are I are tired of talking —

ANTHONY:
I'm tired of hearing *you* talk.

BURGESS:
I let that pass. Let's look at some film.

1. INT NIGHT   A VIENNESE COFFEEHOUSE
Leopold Mozart and his son, Woferl, take coffee in candlelight.
The establishment is cosy, the clientele is musical, the waitresses
bosomy.

LEOPOLD:
A born musician should also be a born mathematician. The two
faculties, for some reason that no doubt Pythagoras has ex-
plained somewhere, spring from an innate numeracy, notes
themselves being vibrations that obey strict mathematical laws.

WOFERL:
But what has mathematics to do with money?

LEOPOLD:
Little perhaps except counting. You have still to get it into your
thick skull that ten Viennese gulden, or florins as it should
rightly be, are worth twelve Salzburg gulden. When you are
offered sums of money for performances you should know precisely what you are getting. A thaler, what the Americans call a
dollar, is two gulden.

WOFERL:
That I knew.

LEOPOLD.
That you knew. But do not confuse a speziesthaler or common

thaler with a reichsthaler. One reichsthaler is worth only one and a half gulden. Three reichsthaler are one ducat and amount to four and a half gulden. And, as you should have remembered from Paris, a Louis d'or or pistole is worth seven and a half gulden. You have to know these things.

WOFERL:
And if I go to Venice?

LEOPOLD:
One Venetian zecchino will be what you will get for five gulden. But you will not be going to Venice. Nor, I think, to London, where they will give you two English shillings for a gulden.

WOFERL:
Money is complicated. Music is simple.

LEOPOLD:
Yes, music is the simple sauce to the gamy meat of a noble or royal or imperial court. And simple servants of the court must purvey it. Break out on your own and you will be cheated. A regular salary, however modest, is to be preferred to the hazards of the itinerant musician's life. As you ought to know.

WOFERL:
I got five watches on the memorable occasion you will remember —

LEOPOLD:
If a thing is memorable it will be remembered.

WOFERL:
I carry them all in case someone thinks of giving me yet another. They all tell different times, else what would be the point of having five?

2. THE SAME THE COFFEEHOUSE STREET DOOR

Dittersdorf enters with difficulty, fighting a blustering wind. A waiter takes his hat and greatcoat. He sees Leopold Mozart and goes over to his table. The camera goes with him. We now see Scene 1 from a different angle. Leopold and his son rise.

LEOPOLD:

Baron von Dittersdorf. You honor us. My son you will know.

DITTERSDORF:

Doubtless, doubtless. To you, I hope, I am still Karl Ditters. Yes, coffee, hot and strong. A bitter night, gentlemen. My present honor cost me one thousand one hundred gulden. Musicians must push themselves upwards in this hard world. And now, in the Bishop's court at Breslau, I am considered too noble to be a musician. I look after His Grace's hounds. I am better known on the hunting field than in the concert hall.

WOFERL:

Congratulations, sir, on possessing the necessary funds to ennoble yourself.

DITTERSDORF:

Do I detect a certain sharpness of tongue? It will not serve you, sir, in the world of music. Nor will any type of talent. I was once a virtuoso violinist, do you know that? I toured Italy under the patronage of the great Gluck.

WOFERL:

Not so great.

DITTERSDORF:

Then I found few opportunities to shine as a soloist. I served in the orchestra of the Court Opera in Vienna here. That is why I am briefly back, to renew old acquaintanceships. Poor devils. I was glad to enter Count Schaffgotsch's service. Security. A modicum of comfort.

LEOPOLD:
You hear, Woferl?

DITTERSDORF:
I see a certain sourness on his lips. Put some sugar in your coffee, sir.

WOFERL:
Silken chains. Perhaps not so silken.

DITTERSDORF:
I have had a modicum of freedom. I have been honored. I played in Bologna and the monks of that city presented me with twenty pounds of candied fruits.

WOFERL:
Will you exchange some of them for four of my watches? Ah, that is the great Muzio Clementi. Brilliant on the keyboard. Tomorrow we will see just how brilliant.

The camera tracks to his hands, which flex themselves athletically.

3. INT DAY VIENNA CONCERT ROOM IN THE
   IMPERIAL PALACE
The fingers flashing on the keyboard that we initially see belong to Clementi. He is playing something flashy of his own. He is flashily attired. The camera pans to the auditors, who include the Emperor Joseph II, the Grand Duke Paul (later to be Czar of all the Russias) and the Grand Duchess Maria Feodorovna. The gathering is brilliant, like Clementi's performance. Mozart, whom we will continue to call Woferl, stands apart, among the higher court servants, decently but cheaply dressed, disdainful, ill at ease. Clementi ends

his piece, to considerable applause. The Emperor rises, with a
scrap of music manuscript paper in his hand.

EMPEROR:
Brilliant, maestro. Now the final test. I have written a few mea-
sures here upon which we would be happy to hear you impro-
vise. A toccata and fugue, perhaps — the fugue in four parts.

CLEMENTI:
Your Imperial Majesty, I will do this with pleasure. But since
Herr Mozart and I are in what we may term friendly competition,
turn and turn about would be in order. I will mop my brow —
with your gracious permission — while he is put through his
paces.

Woferl comes forward, frowning. He frowns more when he reads
the imperial theme.

EMPEROR:
I observe that my little inspiration does not come up to your
exacting standards.

Obsequious laughter.

WOFERL:
An elementary error. The minim in the second bar should be
dotted.

EMPEROR:
Dot it for me, if you think that necessary.

WOFERL:
The rules of music consider it necessary. Not even His Imperial
Majesty is above the law.

The court frowns at his insolence. He sits and plays not merely with technical brilliance but with feeling. The fugue is most intricate but also expressive of deep and complicated emotion. Meanwhile Clementi indulges in a whispered conversation with the Grand Duchess.

CLEMENTI:

The London *cognoscenti*? Gross but appreciative. They have an ear for quality, especially the Jews. But it was at Versailles that I secured my largest triumph. Her Majesty was most gracious — also munificent.

GRAND DUCHESS:

Ah, dear Marie Antoinette. Such taste, such delicacy. And how her subjects adore her.

Clementi wipes his throat with a cambric handkerchief.

GRAND DUKE (*to the Emperor*):
Qu'est-ce que vous pensez?

EMPEROR:
Fabelhaft. Aber —

He makes a gesture indicative of distaste at the complexities, the lack of pure melody.

GRAND DUKE:
Da da, ya ponimaiu.

Woferl finishes his improvisation. The applause is polite but not overenthusiastic. Woferl stands, bows. The Emperor graciously approaches him.

EMPEROR:
Our native Teutonic talent is, you will agree, meritorious. Naturally we bow down to the genius of Italy —

CLEMENTI (*modestly*):
Your Imperial Majesty is too kind.

WOFERL:
He referred, signore, to the national genius. Not to any specific music pedlar.

EMPEROR:
The national genius, yes. We pay our homage to the mother of the arts. Mozart here will, I know, open his ears to what our dear Clementi is about to do with my humble theme.

WOFERL (*muttering*):
He's only a damned mechanic.

EMPEROR:
I beg your pardon? Yes, we look forward to his spiritualizing of a mere machine. Talking of machines —

He produces a large, loudly ticking watch.

Your reward, Mozart. Even our dear Clementi was impressed.

Woferl takes the gift bitterly. He takes from his pocket five watches made, with red ribbon, into a ticking bundle.

WOFERL:
Am I not lucky? Now I have one for each day of the working week. On Sunday, of course, I pass out of time into eternity. I thank Your Imperial Majesty.

He bows sardonically and walks out. The court makes head ges-
tures expressive of sad distaste at such boorishness. Clementi
bows in a superior way and sits at the keyboard. All applaud be-
fore he even starts to play.

4. INT DAY SALZBURG LEOPOLD MOZART'S HOUSE
Leopold is angry, his son excited.

WOFERL:
The chance is there — the great chance, I would say. O'Reilly in
London offers six months, December to June. Three hundred
pounds sterling, which in Salzburg currency is —

LEOPOLD:
Three thousand gulden.

WOFERL:
Two operas, he says. I'm there as a composer, not a mere execu-
tant. Take the two children, that's all I ask.

LEOPOLD:
So you and Constanze fatten yourselves on roast beef while I
grow thin with the worry of looking after your squalling brats.
No. You left His Grace's employ to make your home in Vienna.
And now you're dissatisfied with Vienna.

WOFERL:
I love Vienna but I love money more. I want to travel. That's the
only way to prosper. Please look after the children. Only six
months.

LEOPOLD:
At the end of which I may be dead or you may be dead and two
howling orphans will be thrust onto the street. No. If you must
go, take the children with you.

WOFERL:
Constanze thinks it will be bad for their health. They're delicate, you know.

LEOPOLD:
Thanks to your lack of parental care.

WOFERL:
Do not give me that. At least I don't make a traveling raree-show of them. My darling little prodigy, and you pocketing the gold and handing out a generous kreuzer to buy sweets with. You're selfish, Father.

LEOPOLD:
Get back to Vienna. I will not be spoken to in that manner.

WOFERL:
Oh, you —

What he cannot find words for he expresses in three or four loud discords on the open fortepiano. Then he stalks out.

5. EXT DAY   POTSDAM   GROUNDS OF THE ROYAL
   PALACE
A coach drawn by four prancing bays travels along an endless inner road from gate to palace entrance. The grounds are superbly kept. It is full summer and the air is alive with birdsong.

6. INT DAY   COACH INTERIOR
Mozart sits with Dittersdorf. Let us drop the Woferl.

DITTERSDORF:
His Majesty plays the violoncello abominably, but you must listen to him with your eyes raised to heaven. Dissimulation, simulation. These are the only practical virtues.

MOZART:
Adding up to one vice — hypocrisy.

DITTERSDORF:
Do you want preferment or do you not?

MOZART:
I want money. I need money.

DITTERSDORF:
There is no ever-open coffer at the Prussian court. The path to
riches is indirect. Follow me, do what I do.

MOZART:
You mean — compose your kind of music?

DITTERSDORF:
Well, yes. Simplify. We Germans are too complex for ears in
love with Italy. Have you sent any compositions on ahead?

MOZART:
Why? To be lost by the imperial courier service?

DITTERSDORF:
I employed a special messenger to convey my six new symphonies to the court. They are probably in rehearsal now. By the
way, be especially respectful to Duport, Reichardt and Naumann. They are influential musicians.

MOZART:
Composers?

DITTERSDORF:
So they consider themselves to be. His Majesty thinks highly
of them.

MOZART:
Their names mean nothing.

DITTERSDORF:
To you, no. To me, little. That is not the point. Ah, we seem to have arrived.

7. EXT DAY   THE PALACE
Mozart and Dittersdorf step out of the coach. A chewing, bald, leering lower servant takes their baggage, grumbling.

SERVANT:
Round the corner, your musicianships.

MOZART:
Not the main entrance?

SERVANT:
Nah, that's for the nobs.

Mozart shrugs, Dittersdorf opens his arms to accept the perennial situation. They follow the servant.

8. INT DAY   A MUSIC ROOM IN THE PALACE
The King is playing the violoncello, not too badly. His music is the well-known Minuet in A Major by Boccherini. Boccherini is there, rubbing his hands like a pawnbroker. Mozart and Dittersdorf stand, listening, expressionless. The Princess of Orange enters, first ebullient, then deferential to the music. The King stops playing. Light applause.

KING:
Dear sister, dear dear sister. Gentlemen — fellow musicians I would say — another royal musician, Her Highness the Princess of Orange.

PRINCESS:
Oh no. A mere pawer and dabbler. (*To Boccherini*) Are you the
composer Mozart?

BOCCHERINI:
Ah no, madame. There he is.

PRINCESS:
Thin. And he wears his own hair. Fear not, sir, that fashion may
return. Well, I had thought of him as fat and jolly. That was a
very jolly opera of yours. *Die Entführung.* Quite a success in
Berlin. Pretty girls and funny Turks. Amusing.

MOZART:
Success is a very abstract property, madame.

PRINCESS:
What can you mean?

MOZART:
I prefer the concrete. Money.

*The word, judging from the faces of the assembly, is considered
vulgar.*

KING:
Don't be mercenary, my boy. The tinkle of gold and silver pieces
is very inferior music. I did not play too badly, what?

DITTERSDORF:
Divinely.

BOCCHERINI:
My humble notes were apotheosized by the royal touch, Your
Majesty.

KING:
Pray, no flattery. Well, not too much.

Obsequious titters, except from Mozart.

Count von Dittersdorf, I think the benefit performance you requested is in order. The opera house and the court musicians
are at your disposal, without payment of course. *Job*, eh? A fine
biblical subject. No scraping of boils, I trust. Realism can be
taken too far.

DITTERSDORF:
God bless Your Majesty. It's an oratorio, by the way. No action.

MOZART:
The scraping of the violins will *simulate* the scraping of boils —
so I assume.

This does not go down well.

9. INT NIGHT   THE OPERA HOUSE
*The King, his sister and the royal entourage applaud in their box.
The camera pans to the distinguished applauding audience. Then
it swings to the stage, where the performers bow, along with the
composers Reichardt and Naumann.*

10. INT NIGHT   THE OPERA HOUSE   BACKSTAGE
*Dittersdorf and the two composers open a bottle of champagne in
celebration of a success which history hardly records.*

REICHARDT:
Well, how did you like *Protesilao*?

DITTERSDORF:
Ravishing. Even the title.

NAUMANN:

Were you able to tell which of us two composed which act?

DITTERSDORF:

Both acts were equally ravishing. It is astonishing that two men of exactly equal genius should combine to produce a work of such ravishing beauty that it will undoubtedly hold the stage for centuries to come.

NAUMANN:

You are too kind.

DITTERSDORF:

I am known for discrimination more than kindness. A harsh critic, gentlemen, melted to rapture by the mellifluity of a masterwork.

REICHARDT:

Well, it was not all honey. There were some dramatic asperities.

DITTERSDORF:

Of course there were, but incredibly beautifully resolved.

NAUMANN:

In which act did you most remark these asperities?

DITTERSDORF:

Oh, in both.

NAUMANN:

Not one more than the other?

DITTERSDORF:

One act was a mirror of the other act.

REICHARDT:

You seem to imply a certain static quality. This, surely, moved —
to climax, to catastrophe, to dénouement.

DITTERSDORF:

I refer to excellence of workmanship, spontaneity of melody. Of
course it moved. I was deeply moved. Ah, here comes the great
Duport. Mozart I think you will know.

*Duport and Mozart appear. Mozart is somewhat grudgingly offered
champagne.*

DUPORT:

*Chers maîtres, chers amis. Mes félicitations. Je n'ai jamais dans
toute ma vie entendu une musique tellement ravissante.*

MOZART:

Come, see sense. Well constructed, well performed. But let's not
throw superlatives around.

DITTERSDORF:

He is like this sometimes, gentlemen. Indigestion, I would say.
The rich food of the Prussian court does not agree with him.
I joke, Mozart, I joke.

DUPORT:

J'opine que notre jeune confrère a des réservations.

MOZART:

Look, Duport, you've earned enough money in the German-
speaking territories to pay them the compliment of speaking
their language. You've put German bread in your mouth. Let
German words come out.

DUPORT:

Qu'est-ce qu'il dit, ce bonhomme?

MOZART:

Ce bonhomme dit that the musicians of the court ought to indulge in a little self-criticism. How can music advance without it? Be honest. What we heard and saw tonight was no more than competent. And what I've heard of the music of the *Kapelle* would make a better musician than you, Herr Reichardt, writhe in shame. Music is a wretchedly difficult discipline. Nothing any of us do is good enough.

NAUMANN:

Speak for yourself, sir.

MOZART:

I at least am not bloated with self-satisfaction. I know how far I have to go.

NAUMANN:

We know how far you have to go — in manners, in deference. Your compositions are too little known in the great world for us to make any assessment of your progress on the road to Parnassus. Listen — someone is playing. An exquisite little air.

We hear the continuo harpsichord in the orchestra pit.

MOZART:

Mine. Written for the Queen. I presume the Queen is playing.

DITTERSDORF:

We must go and pay our respects.

MOZART:

Tell her to pay a little money while you're at it. And tell her that her fingering would be a disgrace to a scullery maid.

He goes.

II. INT NIGHT   THE OPERA HOUSE   THE ORCHESTRA
    PIT

*The Queen of Prussia is playing a piece of extreme simplicity,
though clumsily and with many wrong notes. She has an audience
that swoons with delight. She finishes.*

QUEEN:
There. It is not yet perfect.

THE ASSEMBLY:
Oh, but it is. Absolute perfection. Exquisite. Your Majesty's
playing does honor to the music.

We hear Mozart's voice.

MOZART (*off*):
Grow up!

All turn, astonished.

12. INT NIGHT   THE OPERA HOUSE   THE CENTRAL
    AISLE
Mozart comes down the aisle, upbraiding loudly.

MOZART:
Has it ever struck any of you kings, queens, nobility, that music
is more than an ornament, a toy, the auditory wallpaper that
decorates your idle lives? If you want to approach the deity it
will not be through the muttering of the Mass or the clacking
of the rosary. It will be through music — that language that
reaches higher than the language of prayer, that tenuous golden
chain that links the human soul to the divine essence. To you it is
candy for the ear, a soufflé that you gulp and forget, a glass of
wine that you belch after. But music is a cathedral built by the
hands of the devout to the greater glory of God. Ignoring this,

you are heretical. Being heretical, you are damned. And you know where the damned go. The angels of music hide their faces in shame at tonight's travesty. All right, you flunkies, you need not besmirch your white gloves with my summary ejection. I am going.

He leaves.

13. INT NIGHT   THE ORCHESTRA PIT
The assembly watches Mozart go, most of its members appalled. The Queen, however, is impressed.

QUEEN:
So. I begin to understand. In a rational age we lose priests and gain musicians. Perhaps they should be put into monasteries and summoned to court when we need them. Music for the glory of God. There would be no haggling over money. What do you think, my dear?

KING:
An insolent puppy. He will be thrown out on his oversensitive ear. Still, we musicians are grossly undervalued. He's right there. A little too forceful, though, in his statement of the situation. These people should be seen and not heard — well, you know what I mean.

QUEEN:
He composes very prettily. Shall I try it again?

ASSEMBLY:
Oh do, ma'am. Exquisite. Such a queenly touch.

14. EXT DAY   THE PALACE GROUNDS
A coach drawn by four bays drives away. The summer continues glorious, the birdsong is ecstatic.

15. INT DAY   THE COACH
Mozart and Dittersdorf are seated as before. Dittersdorf is counting gold pieces. His leather moneybag rattles and clinks.

DITTERSDORF:
I had to pay one thousand three hundred gulden for the copying of parts. Still, a profit of two and a half thousand. One must not grumble. I'm sorry you did not like my *Job*.

MOZART:
He did not seem to suffer enough.

DITTERSDORF:
You suffered for him, it seems. You come away with empty pockets. When will you learn?

MOZART:
A musician must not be a cringing servant. I literally vomited at the obsequiousness. We must make our own way.

DITTERSDORF:
You know as well as I that it cannot be done.

Mozart looks gloomily into the future.

16. A MONTAGE
Mozart plays piano concertos. He comes to the end of No. 6 in B-flat (K. 238). The camera pans from his bowing to great applause to the applauding audience. The hall is full. Cut to his playing No. 8 in C (K. 246). The audience is appreciative but smaller. He plays No. 24 in C Minor (K. 491). The hall is nearly empty.

17. INT NIGHT   VIENNA   THE BEDROOM OF THE
      MOZARTS
Mozart is in bed. Constanze walks up and down the candlelit room, a child in her arms, soothing, crooning.

MOZART:
A tooth?

CONSTANZE:
Teething.

MOZART:
A dose of laudanum seems indicated.

CONSTANZE:
I've already given it. She's dropping off now.

MOZART:
Like my concert receipts.

CONSTANZE:
Novelty. Then the novelty wears off. Besides, this is the opera season.

MOZART:
How much do we have still?

CONSTANZE:
Not quite enough to pay the grocer. The butcher has been insolent. He raised a fist like a loin of pork at me. You must get more pupils.

MOZART:
Teaching, I do not compose. Moreover, taking the money in advance kills my desire to teach. Put the child in his cradle —

CONSTANZE:
Her.

MOZART:
Come back to bed. I will think of something.

18. INT DAY THE BURGTHEATER SALLE A MANGER
Raucously, the French opera company finishes a meal and drinks wine. Some spit out the wine with mock vomiting noises. One of the company turns to observe the Emperor passing along the corridor which opens into the royal gardens. He gets up, glass in hand.

19. INT DAY THE BURGTHEATER CORRIDOR
The Frenchman rudely accosts the Emperor.

FRENCHMAN:
Your Majesty, we are unused to such treatment. This wine is abominable. We demand that you change our supplier and arrange for the delivery of wine of a quality appropriate to our status, and indeed, if I may say so —

EMPEROR:
Your race, your nation. Let me taste it. Hm. Good enough for me. If not for you. I suggest you return to France, where, I presume, like everything else, you will find better. My Lord Chamberlain!

The Grand Chamberlain, who is in the imperial train, hurries forward.

GRAND CHAMBERLAIN:
Your Imperial Majesty?

EMPEROR:
Dismiss this entire *corps dramatique*, as it calls itself. Pay them off and send them back to Paris. We are sick of French arrogance. We are sick of French opera.

GRAND CHAMBERLAIN:
Ah, we return to our native variety, sire?

EMPEROR:
We have been putting patriotism before excellence. Let the

man *Singspiel* delight the plebs in the Vienna suburbs. Here in the Burgtheater we shall have Italian opera. It is the best. But not that damned moaning and weeping and killing *seria* stuff.

GRAND CHAMBERLAIN:
Opera buffa only?

EMPEROR:
We need to be entertained, not enlightened.

The imperial train moves on. The Frenchman splutters and throws the dregs of his wine glass in the direction of its departure.

FRENCHMAN:
Canaille!

20. INT NIGHT   THE BURGTHEATER
An opera is in progress. The auditorium candles remain lighted. The audience is not overattentive. There is chatter, flirtation. The opera is not by any composer we know. The composer presides at the harpsichord in the pit. Onstage, a soprano sings a cabaletta and falters on her high notes. Rotten fruit and bad eggs are hurled. A member of the audience stands to inveigh.

MEMBER OF THE AUDIENCE:
Never mind about *her*. Throw something at *him*.

He points an accusatory finger at the cowering composer.

He's a thief. He stole that from Sacchini. Or it might be Paisiello.

The opera continues with difficulty.

21. INT NIGHT   A VIENNESE COFFEEHOUSE
Vicente Martín y Soler takes coffee with Giovanni Paisiello.

SOLER:
Outrageous behavior. Yet it may be taken as enthusiasm. For the genre, that is. There is certainly no indifference.

PAISIELLO:
It's the rage for the ever-new that one finds oppressive. Operas are like newspapers. You know how many I have written?

SOLER:
Twenty would be too much.

PAISIELLO:
Over a hundred. The maw of what you would call the aficionados is insatiable. You, me, Salieri, Cimarosa, Guglielmi, Sarti. And there's Mozart pretending to be an Italian.

SOLER:
Touché.

PAISIELLO:
Oh, you're a Latin. Very nearly an Italian. These Viennese can't tell the difference.

SOLER:
Your *Barbiere di Siviglia* exemplifies our internationalism. A Spanish setting, a French play, an Italian operatization.

PAISIELLO:
Your *Una Cosa Rara* is pure Italy. It's knocked out poor little Mozart's *Nozze di Figaro*. The insolence. Figaro's my property.

SOLER:
The man's an instrumentalist. His woodwind fights the voices. There's a certain talent there, but it's not operatic. Will he last?

PAISIELLO:
Will any of us? And does it matter? Come, we're going to be late for *La Grotta di Trofonio.* Salieri will never forgive us.

22. INT NIGHT   THE BURGTHEATER
Salieri's insipid work is in progress. The camera pans over a moderately attentive audience. It reaches Mozart, who stands gloomily at the back. His inner voice speaks over the unmemorable music.

MOZART (*VO*):
And does it matter? Not to be understood? None of us shall see posterity. There's no advantage in working for the yet unborn. If my music dies with my death, I shall be in no position to complain. Am I serving the age I live in, live in very precariously, or am I serving God? Of God's existence I remain unsure, despite my choral praises. Does God manifest himself in the world in trickles of music? I don't know. The quest for perfection, even when perfection is unwanted. This is the crown of thorns. It cannot be rejected. God or no God, I must avoid blasphemy. I am only a little man whose health is not good and whose coffers are empty. Counting each kreuzer. Wondering whether I can afford the pulling of a tooth. The fingers of my right hand are deformed with the incessant penning of notes. And the true music remains unheard, taunting, demanding birth like a dream child. God help some of us. There are some who need no help.

He looks at the stage, where the opera is coming to an end.

23. INT NIGHT   THE BURGTHEATER   THE STAGE
The final ensemble comes to an end. Tonic and dominant. The audience applauds. Salieri rises from the harpsichord and takes his bow. He smiles. Flowers are thrown.

ANTHONY:

Trivial. Vulgar.

BURGESS:

That always happens when you attempt a popular dramatization of the truth. A deformed posterity speaks for Mozart. The basic facts are genuine enough, however. The scenarist has consulted Dr. Steptoe, Winston Dean. What he tries to say is that time thrashes the wheat out of the dross. The contemporaries of a great genius do not see what they have among them. We, posterity, do not see, unless we are scholars, the ghastly amount of competition the unsung genius must contend against. Who hears Paisiello now? Or Martín y Soler? In their day they were far more popular than Mozart. Mozart's orchestration was too thick, they said. It obscured the voices. *Le Nozze di Figaro* was shamefully vulgar as well as unmelodious. *Don Giovanni* was an outmoded puppet play.

ANTHONY:

Yet there was vitality in the librettos. A good libretto is the armature. It will sustain even mediocre music.

BURGESS:

That can be argued. The greatest dramatist of all time is held, rightly, to be Shakespeare. It would seem logical that the best opera librettos should be based on Shakespeare's plots. But it's bad logic. We have two great Shakespearean operas only, and both are by Boito and Verdi. Consider the number of *Hamlet*s that have appeared briefly in the opera houses. *Hamlet* by Thomas, by Hignard, Heward, Kagen, Machavariani, Searle, Szokolay, Bentiou, Chervinski, Reutter. *Amleto* by Caruso, Andreozzi, Mercadante, Buzzolla, Zanardini, Moroni, Faccio, Zafred. What could be more promising than *Antony and Cleopatra*? Yet who now knows the operas by Kaffka, Yuferov, Malipiero, Bondeville, even Samuel Barber? I say nothing of the *Antonius und Kleopatra* by E. F. von Sayn-Wittgenstein-Berleborg. No composer with such a name could ever be remembered.

ANTHONY:

What Paisiello is made to say in that ridiculous film extract is probably true. In the great age of opera, when operas could be mounted without exorbitant fees, unionized orchestras and striking stagehands, the genre was only a kind of higher journalism. The librettos were the work of hacks. Even Shakespeare was dragged down to the level of his bathetic sources. Boito was nearly unique. Lorenzo da Ponte was the kind of sport that appears once in a century. More. Both Verdi and Mozart were lucky.

BURGESS:

Some god or other smiled, though sardonically. Time would tell when time had already conquered two of eternity's gifted children. But we've said too much about opera. If only we could put into words the excellence of Mozart's not solely operatic achievement. The bicentenary is coming to a close. We've heard nearly everything, and the encomia were all of the wine-tasting variety. Two things have struck, apart from the perfection of form: the absence of vulgarity and the absence of sentimentality. Was he just fortunate in living in an age when neither of these two vices had yet come into existence? God knows we're saturated with them now.

ANTHONY:

The term "sentimental" was invented in the Age of Reason. Sterne's *A Sentimental Journey*, the cultivation of feeling and so on. But "sentimental" was merely the adjectival form of "sentiment." To feel is as human as to think. "Sentimentality" is sentiment divorced from its object, enjoyed *in vacuo*. We weep over a sparrow dead in the snow and revel in the weeping. We are filled with sorrow at the news of the victims of an earthquake or a famine and are inwardly delighted that we don't have to do anything about it. To weep over someone dying of thirst when we have a water bottle which we won't unstopper is the extreme of the vice. To alleviate the thirst would be to deprive ourselves of a pleasurable emotion. To enjoy an emotion without being forced to purge the emotion in action — that's sentimentality. As music stirs up emotion unrelated to action, most music has to be sentimental. There are exceptions — Handel, for instance.

BURGESS:

Sentimentality, I would say, is what is aroused by stock devices. There are certain musical devices that draw tears. A supertonic suspension in Elgar, whose works belong to a debased age. The vibrato in Mendelssohn's Violin Concerto, slow movement. Perhaps the *Liebestod* in *Tristan*, where the singer enjoys impending dissolution and love unfulfillable through sex. Mozart never allows emotion to function in a void or to excess. No lingering over melting chords or cadences. The irony of strict form.

ANTHONY:

Is sentimentality an aspect of vulgarity?

BURGESS:

In the sense that sentimentality upsets the human balance, and to be vulgar is to treat a human being as a mere bundle of objects, we may say that they're cognate. The vulgar are usually sentimental, and the sentimental are always vulgar. To turn a human entity into a mere machine that defecates, or an object that arouses lust, or a disembodied appetite for consumer goods — this is vulgarity. It's the essence of contemporary advertising.

ANTHONY:

Why is it in order to admire a woman's breasts and yet vulgar to exclaim over the smashingness of her tits? Both words have the same referent.

BURGESS:

There are degrees of vulgarity. In both instances the part is separated from the whole. There's a degradation in considering a complex human organism as the mere possessor of the means of sexual stimulation. The precious individuality is lost. The connotations of "breast" can, however, be noble and poetic. "Tit," except ornithologically, has only the associations of a debased Oedipal fixation by way of "teat." It half sniggers at the forbidden.

ANTHONY:

In other words, it's vulgar. You speak in circles. Why not merely say that what's vulgar belongs to the *vulgus*, the low, mannerless and uninstructed? I suppose the opposite of the vulgar is the aristocratic. So Mozart's music is aristocratic?

BURGESS:

I see that you take it for granted that he's never vulgar. Which he never is. Vulgarity in music denies the human complexity which supreme art must somehow portray. It makes use of stock devices for suggesting the lower appetites. Trombones can fart and slide. In *Don Giovanni*, as Bernard Shaw says, they conjure a fearful joy. Melodies are compounds of stock progressions and stock cadences. Vulgar music has a smell of the shop-soiled. A jingoistic elation is provoked by a loud, simple tune on the trumpets. Slithering violin tunes are vulgarly sentimental. Introduce irony, as in Erik Satie's *Parade*, and the vulgar is acceptable because it's placed at a distance. To rhyme "love" with "above" is vulgar. It's too easy, it's taking something out of stock. Yes, not even in that overplayed *Rondo à la Turque* is Mozart vulgar. Yes, his music is probably best described as aristocratic. The aristocrat is, by definition, incapable of vulgarity.

ANTHONY:

A supreme irony, when you consider that Mozart was the first of the great composers to attempt revolt against servitude to princes, emperors, archbishops. A man of the middle class asserting a kind of mercantile precursor. We had to wait for Beethoven to hear "I play no longer for such pigs."

BURGESS:

Naturally, I have an idealized image of aristocracy. I've been reading what the English diplomat Henry Swinburne wrote about the table manners of Prince Wenzel Anton Kaunitz, chancellor of state under Maria Theresa, Joseph II and Leopold II, a most able man, apparently. "After dinner, the Prince treated us to the cleaning of his gums; one of the most nauseous operations I have ever witnessed, and it lasted a prodigious long time, accompanied by all manner of noises. He carries a hundred implements in his pocket for this purpose." England has some disgusting aristocrats even now. I won't fall for Evelyn Waugh's curious snobbishness, in which only the titled were to be taken seriously and the rest of us were afflicted with the whine of the underdog. I suppose I mean really the gentleman. All women are ladies, I suppose, so we can ignore the complementary category. And everybody, except in pubs with whimsical vulgarities, is a gentleman when he goes to pump ship. The term is sneered at, the concept is no longer clear. "Remember, my boy, above all a gentleman is gentle." A gentleman is refined, cultivated, and has considerate manners. Mozart is a gentleman in his music, whatever he may have been in private life. Though, despite the legends and the popular dramatizations, I fancy he may have shown gentlemanly qualities enough.

ANTHONY:

This is a mad and totally untenable concept. Are we to judge art in such narrow social terms? We read Shakespeare's *King Lear* and we meet a raging lion. The whole essence of Beethoven and Wagner is their total ungentlemanliness. No music can be gentlemanly music unless it is the discardable vaporings of gentleman amateurs. There is ladylike music too, and some of it was written by gentlemen. But true music is merely human.

BURGESS:

Meaning that it lacks social restraint. It wears its heart on its sleeve. That is vulgar, that is sentimental. Johann Sebastian Bach, the supreme musician, is the truest of gentlemen.

ANTHONY:

A *bourgeois gentilhomme* in danger of boring the public by talking too much about mathematics. A sentimentalist when he gets on to sweet Jesus, all yearning soprano and oboe d'amore.

BURGESS:

Let's stick to Mozart. And let's remember that gentlemanliness is not just outward manners. It's a complex of inner properties, a balanced attitude to life which combines compassion and justice. The justice weighs but does not condemn. Elegance is natural as in a swimming eel or a galloping horse. Feeling is all the more evident because of the steel of the control.

ANTHONY:

Compassion and justice. You make him sound like God Almighty.

BURGESS:

A propos. Let's go back to heaven.

MENDELSSOHN:
Shalom, gentlemen. You've just arrived?

ESH:
Precipitately. We're the Grazioso Quartet of Tel Aviv. I am Chaim Esh, first violin. Efrain Katz, second. Hyam Cohen, viola. Berel Kitaj, 'cello. Naturally, we know who you are. We were rehearsing the Quartet in B-flat — *The Hunt*, as it's called, K. 458 — when a Scud missile struck Berel's apartment. Saddam Hussein, the tyrant of Iraq, launched it. Our instruments were shattered with our bodies. A pity. Bodies are cheap, but not instruments. We were preparing to present all the Mozart quartets in celebration of the bicentenary. The Gulf War came at a bad time. Inopportune. Muslim savagery confronts the distillation of Western culture.

COHEN:
You could say that the bicentenary came at a bad time.

KITAJ:
Bicentennials are decreed by a bland neutrality. But I see what you mean. We'd canceled the trip to Jerusalem in order to rehearse in Tel Aviv. But on the way to Jerusalem we'd probably have had a car crash. An appointment in Samara. Death is neither here nor there. Music remains.

KATZ:
Even without its players?

ESH:
It's in God's head.

KATZ:
I doubt it. The quartets of Mozart were all too human. Civilized conversation between four people in a language above language. The humanity lay in everybody having an equal say. No first fiddle meditating or asserting while the rest plucked or sawed in humble accompaniment. It was what civilization ought to be about.

MENDELSSOHN:
They say that the ingenuity that can create a civilization is the ingenuity that destroys it. The skill that fashions fiddles is the skill that manufactures guns. Anyway, here music is an idea in God's mind, like ourselves. But we have to regret the loss of the crunch of the resined bow, the delicious wavering of the tuning up. Still, you come to a place of no bitterness.

ESH:
Saddam Hussein might at least have not struck us down in the middle of the twentieth bar of the slow movement. There are certain proprieties. But what can Muslims be expected to know of those?

MENDELSSOHN:
There was, then, never any hope of peaceful coexistence?

KATZ:
Could you ever expect Islam to respect Mozart? This Gulf War has, in its very name, a meaning that goes beyond the geographical. There's a great gulf fixed between the cultures. It will never be closed.

MENDELSSOHN:

And yet what ought Mozart to mean to us Jews?

ESH:

Pardon me, you were born a Jew but became a Christian. Or your father did. An apostate, if I may say so.

MENDELSSOHN:

The Nazis reversed the situation. Anyway, Christianity is no more than a Jewish heresy, to be tolerated if not embraced. We are all musicians who idolized the art of a Christian culture. You've probably all played in orchestras accompanying choirs that sang Christian texts.

KATZ:

A Judeo-Christian culture admits tolerance. Or should. This virulent Islam at least rejoices in the gulf that separates it from the West. We don't ever expect to see tolerance there. As for the European tolerance, we're always uneasy. Sometimes I'm uneasy when playing Mozart. A numbness gets into my fingers. It is because of what happened to my father. He was a violinist like myself. He was lashed on the hands for daring to play Mozart. Mozart was a German property, hence Nazi. Sometimes I think we Jews ought to go back to the *toph* and the *nebel*, the *ugab* and the *halil*, whatever they were. We got ourselves Hellenized. We even have to go to a Greek-named place of worship. And to reject harmony and counterpoint and the work of the violin makers of Christian Cremona would be to embrace the barbarism of the Muslims. Even in the Jewish homeland we accept the diaspora.

MENDELSSOHN:

I still cling to the view of the progressive nineteenth century. Western music is the only music capable of expressing universal emotions. But now we have scholars prepared to take seriously the *mathna* and the *mutlaq* and the *sabbaba* and the *wusta* and the rest of the Islamic monstrosities. Such mistunings could never produce a Mozart.

ESH:

On our fiddles there are more than semitones. F-sharp is not G-flat. The future of music may well lie in following barbaric examples. The subtle splitting of the semitone. But we have for the moment to be satisfied with the tempered scale that was good enough for Mozart. We may be children of the Middle East but we accept that we're a transplanted West. What music better expresses what the non-Islamic world stands for than the music of Mozart?

COHEN:

The Koran bans all music.

ESH:

Pardon me, it does not, though it does not recommend it as an attribute of worship. It was the puritanical followers of the Prophet who called the music of instruments a forbidden pleasure. The *jank* or harp and the flute or *nay* or *qussaba*. Those, incidentally, they stole from us, as they stole the cantillation of the Psalms and gave it to the muezzin. They have a sort of music, but it is music without harmony, counterpoint or the heaven of the orchestra as we know it. There is a profound division between the Sons of the Prophet and the Children of the Scriptures, and it is music that cries to God of the division.

MENDELSSOHN:

We have a sort of apartheid here. The Muslims have their own oversensual heaven and even their own God. You are now residents of a more complex heaven. "With thy choir of saints forevermore I shall be made thy music." A Christian wrote that. The prophecy is fulfilled for us all. Do you wish a formal welcome?

KATZ:
Shall we meet Mozart?

MENDELSSOHN:
Eternity is about to pay gracious homage to time. Eternity, as
the poet Blake said, is in love with its products. The musicians of
the world, which means the West, are assembling to hear Mozart
perform. They are coming now, cleansed and sanctified, to take
their seats in this vast auditorium of the heavens. Palestrina, Monteverdi, the murderer Gesualdo, Haydn, Wagner —

ESH:
We don't wish to meet that anti-Semite.

MENDELSSOHN:
There is Beethoven as he was at fifty, slovenly, with gray hair
tangled like his own piano wires, egg yolk on his shirt. He has
some theory about genius being best shown by neglect of appearance. Music is the thing in itself, all the rest is empty phe-
nomenon. We're honored — he comes to stand at the back
with us.

BEETHOVEN:
Newly arrived?

ESH:
Blown sky-high by Muslims.

BEETHOVEN:
So the Turks are at it again. Why a harpsichord and not a
Hammerklavier?

MENDELSSOHN:
Mozart requested it. It has been exquisitely tuned. There are

even celestial candles. Everything is of his period. He will appear in a moment. Not walk on, appear. Look, he appears.

BEETHOVEN:
God, no, no. The vulgarity, the sentimentality —

MENDELSSOHN:
This I did not expect. How old is he? Five? Four? He climbs onto the stool as if it were a hillock.

BEETHOVEN:
Ach, mein Gott — the infant prodigy.

MENDELSSOHN:
And now his father appears, presumably to turn the pages. Strange. It does not seem to be Leopold Mozart.

BEETHOVEN:
Oh God.

MENDELSSOHN:
Precisely.

Epilogue

I ADDRESS the reader as an integrated person, not one whimsically split into two. I have tried to dramatize; now I must try to be lyrical.

When we were young, a lot of us were rather sour about Mozart. We were jealous about his having so much talent and disclosing it at so early an age. Ordinary young people care little for infant prodigies. We were told that his ear was so sensitive that he fainted at the sound of a trumpet, and that his sense of pitch was so acute that he could distinguish a fifth from a sixth of a tone. He composed pretty little things at the age of four and played like an angel on the harpsichord. Complimented by the Empress Maria Theresa, he leapt onto her lap and kissed her. So charming, with his little wig and his brocade and silk stockings. A milksop.

Even as a young man, I found it difficult to fit Mozart into my sonic universe. I was not alone in that. The reputation of Mozart is now at its highest and will presently suffer a reaction, but he was no demigod in the 1930s. Musicians like Edward Dent and Sir Thomas Beecham had much to do with the promotion of a periwigged historical figure into a voice of the Western civilization that was under the threat from the very race of which Mozart was a member (Salzburg, his birthplace, was an independent city-state; he never saw himself as an Austrian national). It was necessary to hear a good deal of Mozart, and this was not easy. One could, of course, play the keyboard pieces, but, to a piano pupil or a self-taught pianist like myself, there was little that was attractive in the scale passages one fumbled over, or in the conventional tonic-dominant cadences. A boy born into the age of Schoenberg's *Pierrot Lunaire* and Stravinsky's *Le Sacre du Printemps* (I was born five years after the first, four years after the other) found it hard to be tolerant of the Mozartian blandness.

One great war and the threat of another justified barbaric dissonance and slate-pencil-screeching atonality. I needed the music of my own time — Hindemith, Honegger, Bartók. In the Soviet Union Mossolov produced his *Factory* and *Dnieper Power Station*, and those banal chunks of onomatopoeia at least spoke of the modern world. The symphony orchestra had, following Wagner and Richard Strauss, evolved into a virtuoso complex capable of anything. Mozart had been unlucky with his valveless horns and trumpets: he had been enclosed by the technically primitive. So, anyway, it seemed.

I wanted modernity, but where did modernity begin? Probably with Debussy's *L'Après-midi d'un Faune*, which had entranced my ear when, as a boy of thirteen, I had fiddled with the cat's whisker on my homemade crystal set, heard a silence punctuated by a cough or two, and then was overwhelmed by that opening flute descending a whole tritone. This was as much the new age as Mossolov's machine music: it denied the hegemony of tonic and dominant, exalted in color, wallowed in sensuality. Debussy promised a full meal, well sauced. Mozart offered only bread and water.

The appetite for the modern did not exclude the ancient. I read Peter Warlock's study of Gesualdo, *Musician and Murderer*, and was led to the perusal of madrigals I was not yet permitted to hear. The harmonic sequences looked hair-raising. The seventeenth century was closer to my own epoch than the ages in between. Henry Purcell broke the rules that the textbooks were eventually to make petrific. The baroque was acceptable if it meant Bach and Handel. Ezra Pound was yet to resurrect Vivaldi. Stravinsky had sounded the "Back to Bach" call, and the composer of *Le Sacre* could do no wrong. But this was, as Constant Lambert was to point out in *Music Ho!*, sheer evasion. Stravinsky was a "time traveler," prepared to go anywhere so long as it was not in the direction of neo-romanticism. To Stravinsky there was something salutary in clockwork rhythms, the inexpressive deadpan, an eschewing of the dynamic. But true baroque was something different.

Its charm lay in its exaggeration, and Bach's counterpoint went too far. It imposed on the listener the task of hearing many voices at the same time. The effect was of intellectual rigor, and intellectual rigor was, in a curious way, analogous to physical shock. The approach to both the baroque and the modern was not by way of the emotions. Romantic music, reaching its apogee in *Tristan and Isolde*, depended on its capacity to rend the heart. Young people distrust emotion, indeed are hardly capable of it unless it takes the form of self-pity. Sir Thomas Beecham promoted Delius as much as Mozart, and the death-wish element in *The Walk to the Paradise Gardens* was acceptable to the misunderstood young.

But why this rejection of Mozart, the charming but unromantic, the restrained, the formal? He seemed too simple, too scared of the complex. He made neither an intellectual nor a physical impact. Bach, after a day's slaving at six-part counterpoint, would say: "Let's go and hear the pretty tunes." He meant plain sweet melody with a chordal accompaniment. He was not disparaging such art but he recognized that it was diversion more than serious musical engagement. It was an art waiting to be turned into Mozart.

Looming behind modernism, but in a sense its father, there was the personality of Ludwig van Beethoven. My benighted age-group accepted the Beethoven symphony as a kind of musical ultimate, something that the composers of our own age could not aspire to because they had been forced into abandoning the key-system on which it was based. The key-system was worn out; it could linger in the dance or music hall, but modernity

meant either a return to the Greek or folk modes, as with Bartók
or Vaughan Williams, or the total explosion of tonality. Atonal-
ism recognized no note of the chromatic scale as being more
important than any other, but the diatonic scale that was good
enough for Beethoven had a hierarchical basis: number 1 of the
scale, the tonic, was king; number 5, the dominant, was queen;
number 4, the subdominant, was jack or knave. It spoke of a
settled past, but Beethoven was not always easy in it. His sonatas
and symphonies were dramas, storm and stress, revelations of
personal struggle and triumph. The messiah from Bonn, of
whom Joseph Haydn, not Mozart, was the prophet, belonged to
a world that was striving to make itself modern. Beethoven
moved forward; Mozart stayed where he was.

The term "rococo" got itself applied to Mozart's music, and
the associations were of prettiness, sugary decorativeness, a
dead end of diversion. We were not listening carefully enough to
his Symphony No. 40 in G Minor. We heard pleasing sounds
but we were not conscious of a language. If we talk of a musical
language at all, it must be only in a metaphorical sense, but there
was an assumption that Beethoven and his successors were send-
ing messages while Mozart was merely spinning notes.

Music can only properly have meaning when language is imposed upon it, as in song, opera, oratorio or other vocal genres,
or when language is applied laterally — in the form of a literary
program, as in Strauss's tone poems. And yet we assume that in-
strumental music has meaning: it is organized, as language can
be, to an end that, if not semantic, is certainly aesthetic, and it
produces mental effects as language does. It differs from the
other arts, and spectacularly from literature, in being nonrepre-
sentational. Limited to metaphorical statements of a sort, it can
only have a semantic content through analogy.

As Ezra Pound pointed out, poetry decays when it moves too
far away from song, and music decays when it forgets the dance.
In the music of the eighteenth century it may be said that the
spirit of the dance was raised to its highest level. That spirit pro-

gressively deteriorated in the nineteenth century, and in the music drama of Wagner it may be said to have yielded to the rhythms of spoken discourse. Paradoxically, in a work specifically intended for ballet, the dance spirit seems to have been liquidated. *Le Sacre du Printemps* reduces the dance to prehistoric gamboling unsure of its steps. But with Haydn, Mozart and Beethoven we hear a fusion of dance and sonata form and, in the traditional third-movement minuet, the invocation of a specific dance form. But these dance movements are not intended for the physical participation of dancers. The dance becomes an object of contemplation and, in so being, takes on a symbolic function.

The dance as a collective activity, whether in imperial courts or on the village green, celebrates the union of man and woman and that larger union known as the human collective. The Haydn or Mozart symphony asks us to take in the dance in archetypal tempi — moderately rapid, slow, furiously rapid, two or three or four to the bar — and meditate on their communal significance. The sonata or the string quartet or the concerto or the symphony becomes symbolic of human order. With Mozart it seems evident that the more or less static tranquility of the Austro-Hungarian Empire is being celebrated. Thus the music is objective, lacks any personal content of a Mahlerian or Straussian kind, and through that irony which is a corrective to the complacency of social order, works through the alternation of stress and resolution. The heart is the organ that it imitates, but it is the heart of the community. There may be a modicum of personal inflection of the objective structure — comic in Haydn, pathetic in Mozart — but any large incursion of idiosyncratic symbols has to be resisted. In Mahler banal barrel-organ tunes may grind because of adventitious associations, but the Mozart symphony remains aloof from such egotistical intrusions.

It seemed in my youth that the Austro-Hungarian Empire was hopelessly remote. It had collapsed in World War I; before that collapse Freud and Schoenberg recorded the turmoil of individual psyches, microcosms of a larger confusion. It was easy to forget that, in respect of its art, that empire was still with us. A failed Viennese architect was to tyrannize Europe; in the Adriatic port of the empire James Joyce began to revolutionize world literature; Rainer Maria Rilke affirmed poetic modernity in the *Duino Elegies*. And, of course, in music atonality and serialism portended a major revolution. Everything happened in Vienna. If Mozart seemed to stand for a kind of imperial stasis, yet it ought to have been clear to the close listener that a chromatic restlessness was at work and that, within accepted frameworks, the situation of an individual soul, not an abstract item in the citizenry, was being delineated. Mozart was as Viennese as Freud.

I must beware of overpersonalizing an art that manifests its individuality in ways of managing pure sound. One aspect of Mozart's greatness is a superiority in disposing the sonic material that was the common stock of composers of his time. Sometimes he sleeps, nods, churns out what society requires or what will pay an outstanding milliner's bill, but he is never less than efficient. Clumsiness is sometimes associated with greatness: the wrestling, not always successfully, with new techniques. Mozart is never clumsy; his unvarying skill can repel romantic temperaments. "Professionalism" can be a dirty word. He touched nothing that he did not adorn. If only, like Shakespeare, he had occasionally put a foot wrong — so some murmur. He never fails to astonish with his suave or prickly elegance.

It is his excellence that prompts disparagement. The perfection of his work has perversely inspired denigration of his personality. There is a mostly fictitious Mozart whom it is convenient to call Amadeus — a name he was never known to use. This is the man whom an equally fictitious Salieri wished to kill from a variety of motives: clear-headed recognition of his excellence stoking jealousy, the horror of the disparity between his genius and a scatomaniacal infantilism, a Christian conviction of the diabolic provenance of his skill. This makes compelling drama but bad biography. In personal letters the whole Mozart family discloses a delight in the scatological — harmless, conventional, not untypical of an Age of Reason that gained pleasurable shocks from the contrast between the muckheap of the body and the soaring cleanliness of the spirit. All the evidence shows a Mozart who obeyed most of the rules of Viennese propriety, accepting the God of the Church and the Great Architect of the Freemasons. An attempt to mythologize Mozart's end — the mysterious stranger with the commission to compose a Requiem, the pauper's grave, the desertion of the coffin in a sudden storm — collapses under scrutiny of the recorded facts. Meteorological records, the imperial decree to cut down on funeral expenses through the use of common graves, the not uncommon plagiarisms of amateur musicians with more money than talent, melt the mythology into banality. The heresy of indecorous probing into an artist's life has been with us for a long time. Few can take their art straight.

I began my artistic career as a self-taught composer who, because of insufficient talent and a recognition that music could not say the things I wished to say, took, almost in middle age, to the practice of a more articulate craft. Yet the musical background will not be stilled, and the standards I set myself owe more to the great composers than to the great writers. It has always seemed to me that an artist's devotion to his art is primarily manifested in prolific production. Mozart, who produced a great deal of music in a short life, knew that mastery was to be attained only through steady application. His literary counterparts — Balzac in France, Wells and Bennett in England — have often been reviled for what is termed "overproduction." To discover virtue in costiveness was a mark of Bloomsbury gentility. Ladies and gentlemen should be above the exigencies of the tradesman's life. But art is a trade that ennobles itself, and the consumer, by giving more than is paid for. The market is served but also God. Mozart wrote for money, which E. M. Forster did not have to do: his scant production is appropriate to a *rentier* as Mozart's fecundity is right both for a serious craftsman and a breadwinner. Ultimately artists must be judged not merely by excellence but by bulk and variety. The musician is, however, luckier than the writer: it is always possible to produce an acceptable minuet, rather more difficult to achieve a story or a poem.

Literature, in the form of the text to be set to music, must always be ready to help the composer; whether music can help literature is another matter. Earlier in this inadequate centennial tribute, the reader will find a kind of fiction whose structure is derived from Mozart's Fortieth Symphony in G Minor. There is a vague male essence and a vague female, at first disjunct because the principle of key, taken shamefully literally, separates them, later permitted to consummate marriage through the occupation of the room of a common tonality. The figure on the carpet is the persistent quaver accompaniment of Mozart's main, or male, theme in the first movement. The pervading melancholy is that of a minor key. The minuet is too fast and too sad for more than a bizarre and impossible ball. In the last movement there is expected and long-awaited dissolution. The symphonization of fiction is shown to be an implausible undertaking, but things have occasionally to be done to show that they cannot be done. The celebration of Mozart cannot be accomplished in words, except those of stringent technical analysis with ample music-type illustration. We can only celebrate by listening massively and then emitting some almost preverbal noise of approval, amazement or exaltation. But, to the artist in whatever medium, Mozart presents an example to be followed, that of devotion to craft. Without craft there can be no art.

Those of us who practice, as I still inadequately do, the craft of music cannot easily stifle envy. It is not envy of individual genius so much as a bitterness that the cultural conditions which made Mozart possible have long passed away. The division between the music of the street and that of the salon and opera house was not so blatant as it now is. Bach could end his Gold-berg Variations with a quodlibet based on the popular tunes of his day. Conversely, melodies from Mozart's operas could be whistled, and not solely by aristocrats dressing for dinner. Till quite recently the ghost of the sense of a musical community lingered. A Mozart sonata could be popularized, though condescendingly, as "In an Eighteenth-Century Drawing Room"; Frank Sinatra, in his earliest film, could sing *Là ci darem la mano*. Simple tuneful melody was something of a constant. Stravinsky tried to make money by converting a theme from *L'Oiseau de Feu* into a pop ballad. But what was popularized came from the classical or romantic past: no music by Schoenberg, Webern or Bartók could hope to entrance the general ear. The gulf between the serious and the merely diverting is now firmly fixed.

A serious composer commissioned to write, say, an oboe concerto will feel dubious about using tonality with occasional concords; he is uneasy about critical sneers if he does not seem to be trying to outdo Pierre Boulez. There are various modes of musical expression available, perhaps too many, but none of them can have more than a tenuous link with the past. Atonality, polytonality, polymodalism, postmodality, Africanism, Indianism, minimalism, Cageism — the list is extensive. No composer can draw on the heritage that united Monteverdi and Mozart. Alban Berg, in his Violin Concerto, could quote Bach's chorale *Es Ist Genug* only because its tritonal opening bar fitted, by accident, into his tone row. Perhaps only the neurotic Mahler, last of the great tonal Viennese, provides the bridge between a dead and a living society. Mozart can be parodied or pastiched, as in Stravinsky's mannered *The Rake's Progress*, but we cannot imagine his wearing a lounge suit, as we can imagine Beethoven coming back in stained sweater and baggy flannels.

We have to beware of approaching Mozart while polishing the spectacles of historical perspective. Nostalgia is behovely, but it is inert. The vision he purveys must not be that of a long-dead stability for which we hopelessly yearn. In a world which affronts us daily with war, starvation, pollution, the destruction of the rain forests, and the breakdown of public and domestic morality, we may put a Mozart string quartet on the cassette player in the expectation of a transient peace. But it is not Mozart's function to soothe: he is not a tranquilizer to be taken out of the cupboard. He purveys an image of a possible future rather than of an irrecoverable past.

As a literary practitioner I look for his analogue among great writers. He may not have the complex humanity of Shakespeare, but he has more than the gnomic neatness of an Augustan like Alexander Pope. It would not be extravagant to find in him something like the serenity of Dante Alighieri. If the paradisal is more characteristic of him than the infernal or even the pur-gatorial, that is because history itself has written *The Divine Comedy* backwards. He reminds us of human possibilities. Dead *nel mezzo del cammin di nostra vita* he nevertheless presents the whole compass of life and intimates that noble visions exist only because they can be realized.